Ashes
and a Thunderstorm

A New Reading of the Book of Job

Craig Bingham

Araphel Publishing

Ashes and a Thunderstorm
Copyright © 2022 by Craig Bingham

Interior illustrations copyright © 2022 by Hanna Bingham
Cover design by Hanna Bingham, created by Craig Bingham

Araphel Publishing
www.araphel-publishing.com

Library of Congress Control Number: 2022902305

ISBN (paperback) 979-8985604207

For all who have lived a part of Job's story:
may his ending be yours as well.

And for Hanna,
without whom this book would not exist.

Contents

Introduction

When it comes to the Jewish and Christian scriptural texts, the book of Job is *the* classic portrayal of suffering and spiritual transformation. Inexplicable suffering is a pervasive reality of the human experience, and for a life of faith poses a troubling question: how does one reconcile belief in a good God with the actual experience of suffering and evil in this world? In answer to this question, the anonymous author of the book of Job crafted an incredible story—a text referred to by modern literary critic and biblical scholar Robert Alter as "arguably the greatest achievement of all biblical poetry."[1] In an apt tribute to the subject matter, the Hebrew scriptures reserve for the topic of human suffering their most daring piece of literary artistry. Instead of avoiding the difficult issue, the anguish of Job is placed front and center, dealt with through exquisite, shocking, and heart-wrenching poetry.

In addition to the unsurpassed breadth of its poetic scope, the book of Job also stands out within the Hebrew scriptures in terms of genre, perhaps best classified as the sole literary epic of that collection. It is a story that follows its hero, Job, through his trials and tribulations as he wrestles with undeserved suffering and the nature of humanity's relationship with God. Job is an

1

unusual protagonist for a literary epic, exhibiting virtually none of the traits present in other famous heroes from cultures near ancient Israel. He is no crafty and competent Odysseus fighting and scheming to return home, nor is he a warrior-king like Gilgamesh seeking the secrets of immortality. The very differences in style and focus between the book of Job and other epics from cultures surrounding ancient Israel emphasize its striking uniqueness. Job is no superhuman Hercules, nor is he a shapeshifter or demigod with supernatural abilities fighting evil monsters or demons; instead, he is an ordinary and upright man who faces realistic (if extreme) losses and persists in his faith. For Israel, the people of the covenant, the heroic arc was portrayed not by conquering fantastical creatures, outwitting the gods, or even—as will be seen in the story itself—winning out in some divinely ordained contest involving a test of character. In the book of Job an unusual heroic arc is portrayed, as Job confronts the agonizing questions of faith, encounters God, and is transformed. By the end of the book, Job has encountered the God of creation and of life, and that encounter has left him changed in profound ways.

I have written this book as a reflection on the story of Job, particularly to address what I see as a significant issue in the way it is commonly read. My underlying premise is that the book of Job was composed with an intentionally mirrored structure, its two halves reflecting and informing one another. To miss this central fact, and the interplay between the two halves of the story, is to miss the profound depths of artistry in Job and to misread it as a piece of literature. Instead of reading Job through the lens of a two-part mirrored structure, most interpretations read the book in a linear fashion, a perspective that leaves lingering questions about troubling aspects of the story. How is one supposed to interpret the callousness involved in Job's initial test of faith, a test with extensive collateral damage that seems unimportant to an apparently unfeeling God? What is one supposed to do with the apparent irrelevance of God's speeches at the end of the book, or the seemingly glib restoration of Job's children and wealth which concludes the narrative?

The book of Job is not a story that was meant to be read linearly. Like so much of Hebrew poetry, it was meant to be read with an eye to statement and re-statement, articulation and echo. In the first half of the book the author introduces certain problematic but common perspectives on suffering—the idea that suffering is part of a divine test of faith, or that suffering is retribution for sin of some kind—that are then undermined and ultimately deconstructed as the story progresses. The second half of the book involves an elegant reconstruction of those initial themes and perspectives, but in a radically transformed way, drawing the reader or listener into a profound shift in perspective and understanding that provides the author's true answer to the issue of suffering. My recommendation to the reader of my book is to read through it as a whole in order to keep the ideas and themes fresh as they develop and shift. The main body of the book follows Job's story as it unfolds, while the afterword then reflects on the book of Job from within our modern context. This book is not written like a commentary with reflections on each verse or chapter in isolation; it is an attempt to frame the book of Job in the context of its mirrored structure, in which the events and perspectives from the beginning of the book are illuminated and even reinterpreted by their mirrored counterparts at the end of the story.

Unless otherwise noted, all translations from the book of Job are my own. Admittedly, providing an adequate translation for any part of Job in English is a virtually impossible task, and I make no presumptions about the translations I have given; I simply enjoyed the challenge of wrestling with the text to approximate something of the dynamic artistry of the poet. Although I generally attempt to preserve something of the original Hebrew syntax and wording where possible, I have chosen in some instances to err on the side of paraphrase for the sake of clarity. I have also chosen to emphasize multi-line stanzas in the layout of the text, rather than the continual pairing of two or three lines, and have adopted a free verse or even fractured style, particularly when it comes to Job's speeches, because I believe that it is a form of poetry with more potential for conveying the artistry of the text and the agony of Job.

Human suffering, the primary concern of the book of

Job, remains as prevalent today as it was two and a half millennia ago. Most of this book took shape in 2020 and 2021, years filled with catastrophes, the most notable being the Covid-19 pandemic that ravaged the world, killing millions, fracturing communities, disrupting global economic systems, and leaving many facing unknown long-term effects. Disease, human violence, and natural disasters occur in our world with depressing regularity, giving rise in our day to the same kinds of experiences and questions that drive the narrative of the book of Job. Beyond the massive earth-shaking catastrophes which fill the news headlines, there also exist the constant small and individual sufferings which make up the everyday, ubiquitous nature of life in our world. It is to all these realities of suffering and struggle, great and small, to which the story of Job was written, and to which I hope this book, reflecting on Job, can speak a good word.

Part One:
Ashes

1

The words of Job are ended

"The words of Job are ended."
Job 31:40 (NIV)

It may seem odd to begin in the middle of the book of Job, with words that would be well-suited to conclude a story. This phrase from the end of chapter thirty-one about the end of Job's words, though, places the reader or listener at a unique vantage point, from which it is possible to see the mirrored structure of the book unfolding in both directions. The fact that this phrase does not end the book of Job is surprising. Even more surprising, it is followed by more words from Job. The statement about the end of Job's words is a comment made by the story's narrator, bringing the flow of the narration to a complete stop. After the shock of Job's experiences of suffering and the fervor of passionate and heated speeches between Job and his three friends, the author steps in and causes the events of the story to pause and slide into silence. Structurally speaking, this is a critical moment; it is the central hinge on which the narrative turns. On either side of these words are two halves of the story which mirror one another in surprising and unexpected ways.

In the silence the scene unfolds: Job is center stage, sitting on an ash-heap with a piece of broken pottery in his hand which he is using to scrape his painful sores. The ashes and the broken pottery are symbolic of his shattered life, as he has just witnessed the inexplicable destruction of virtually all he holds dear—his property stolen by raiders, his children killed by natural disasters, and his body wasted and wrecked by the sudden onset of painful disease. Seated around him are three of his friends, each of whom made a lengthy journey to be with him in his distress. The silence at this particular moment, though, is not one of comfort or consolation, but one that is sharp with anger and resentment. Job has just finished making the most severe oath imaginable in defense of his innocence, putting God on trial for the devastation of his life and rejecting the explanations and cautionary advice offered by his friends. It is easy to picture Job's friends unsure of what to do or say in response to his impassioned protestations, hurt by Job's rebuff of their advice and angry at his blasphemous case against God.

The first half of the book—half in terms of structure, not in measure of length—is comprised of a series of events that together propel the narrative to this point of fractured, painful silence. This moment, frozen in time for us briefly by the author, is the culmination of the first half of the book, the end of human wisdom and Job's expression of his suffering. Knowing where the author is heading will help in following the twists and turns of the plot. Every thread of Job's story in the first half of the book is drawn toward this central image, to this scene of fractured silence around an ash-heap, and the "end" of Job's words.

2

A double misdirection
Job 1-2

There once was a man in the land of Uz—his name was Job.
    Job 1:1a

The book of Job opens to a scene quite different from the ash-heap and angry silence of chapter thirty-one. In the very first line of the book we are drawn into an ancient and distant world in a mysterious land called Uz. Job's introduction as a character is comprised of a few short lines, where he is described as prosperous, righteous, and materially blessed, living what the people of his time would have thought to be the ideal existence for a human being:

He lived with integrity, and was a righteous man, fearing God and shunning evil. Children were born to him, seven sons and three daughters, and he had seven thousand sheep, three thousand camels, five hundred pairs of oxen, five hundred donkeys, and a very large household. He was the greatest of all the people of the east.

Job 1:1b-3

The description of Job's life is brief but symbolically rich. He is a righteous man, and he lives with integrity, fearing God and turning away from evil, descriptions which comprise a fourfold list with symbolic overtones of completeness. In each instance the specific numbers of Job's children and animals add up to multiples of ten, reflecting both a sense of completeness and balanced harmony within each aspect of his life. Because of this, Job is aptly described as *"the greatest of all the people of the east."* Though Job's introduction is short, the author's symbolic use of number to convey harmony and completeness gives a figurative sense of Job's blessed life.

The Hebrew word for "east" used in Job's opening description, *qedem*, is a word with more layered complexity than our modern indicator of cardinal direction. In Hebrew, the language of ancient Israel, some of the words for direction and time overlapped. Time and space were generally oriented from the perspective one would have if standing on the lowland coastal plains facing east, with the Mediterranean Sea behind and the eastern foothills ahead. Because of the linguistic overlap in time and space, *qedem* can mean both "east" and "before." The English term "before" is actually a fitting parallel, because it can be used with similar ambiguity. It is possible to talk about something that happened "before your very eyes" (spatial), or to reference something that happened "before you were born" (temporal). For the conceptual ancient Israelite figure, the past stretched out before them toward the east, the origin of the rising sun and the hazy depths of times before; the future lay behind them, toward the sea, yet unseen and unknown.

Because of this linguistic ambiguity and difficulty in translation, it is easy to miss an important aspect of the story's framing. Job is called the greatest of all the people of the east—greatest of all the people who live geographically to the east of Israel, which is where the ancient city of Uz is assumed to have been, but also hinting subtly at Job's status as the greatest of all those who have come before, all past ancestors. Job's introduction is not meant to set the story up as a work of fiction like we would think of it today, but as a tale that happens in another time and place, long ago and far away, with the figure of Job casting a long shadow on the rest of history as an exemplar of faith, suffering, and transformation.

After the initial introduction focused on Job's complete and harmonious life, there is a description of his daily pattern of actions. Again, the description is brief and symbolically rich in meaning, meant to serve as a paradigmatic example of his character and personality:

His sons would hold feasts in their homes, each one on his day, and they would invite their three sisters to eat and drink with them. When the days of feasting would end, Job would send and sanctify them. He would rise early and sacrifice burnt offerings for each one, for Job said, "Perhaps my sons have sinned, and blessed God in their hearts." This was Job's regular practice.

Job 1:4-5

Job is religiously diligent to the point of scrupulousness. He rises early in the morning and provides burnt offerings for his children on the mere possibility that one of them has sinned in the secrecy of their own hearts. Job is faithful to his religious obligations, regularly going above and beyond the normal expectations of a religious life. With this description of Job's religious practice, his character has been rounded out for us as readers and listeners: a complete and harmonious life, the greatest of all the people of the east, and religiously diligent to an extreme.

After this brief introduction to the character of Job, the plot of the story begins to unfold. Tragic events, orchestrated from heaven and framed as a test of human faithfulness, occur in a series of escalating crises as Job suffers terrible loss and physical torment, setting the stage for the rest of the book and the theme of human suffering. It might be helpful to visualize the story of Job as a deep valley with a path heading down into it, inviting the reader or listener to enter the depths of suffering with Job. Right now, we would be standing beside Job at the beginning of the path, right on the valley's edge, looking down into the shadowed depths. The fractured silence at the end of chapter thirty-one would serve as the low point of this valley, the place from which all seems dark and hopeless. It is only by journeying down into the valley with Job, though, that there is the possibility of a surprising revelation of God and of moving forward into renewed life. Though too far away to see properly, the far side of the valley is where the path that takes Job into new life is found.

The image of a valley also fits with the two-part mirrored structure of the book. Compositionally speaking, the fact that there are two halves to the story that mirror and reflect one another is not surprising in a text from ancient Israel, since the pairing of lines is one of the most foundational forms of poetry in the Hebrew scriptures. Ideas or images are echoed in subsequent lines, perhaps further advancing an image or theme from the initial line or juxtaposing something unexpected and seemingly contradictory. In some ways, the book of Job is like a poetic couplet writ large, the two halves of the book intentionally complementing and contrasting one another. The very paradigm for understanding the experience of suffering and the nature of the relationship between humanity and the divine undergoes a radical shift which is reflected in the two different halves of the story. The first half of the book contains the author's set-up, creating a particular framework of understanding which will be brought into tension, deconstructed, and then rearticulated in an utterly transformed way in the second half of the book.

Because of the complexity involved in this kind of mirroring, the image of Job as a poetic couplet writ large is overly simplistic. Turning more broadly to literary theory, a method of writing closely related to this kind of deconstruction and rearticulation is a storytelling device known as *misdirection*. An author using narrative misdirection initially draws a reader or listener into a particular paradigm of interpretation, only to subvert that paradigm in an unexpected reversal of perspectives later in the book. One of the most common and easily recognizable modern uses of misdirection occurs in certain mystery novels. In a classic "whodunit" mystery novel, the author engages with the reader in a game of sorts by dropping enough subtle clues that the reader is able (theoretically) to solve the mystery as it unfolds. However, a skillful author diverts the reader's attention into a certain paradigm of interpretation in such a way that it is only at the end of the novel that everything falls into place in a climactic scene, the classic "aha!" moment. That "aha!" moment is when the initial paradigm of understanding is shattered, either by new information or a new perspective of some kind, and all the previous events of the story fall into place in a new and more profound way. There is something deeply satisfying about looking back over a story while viewing it from the vantage point of new information that completely changes the way it is understood. It is, moreover, a powerful literary tool for an author who is trying to cause a paradigm shift within a reader or listener.

The author's use of misdirection in the unfolding narrative of the book of Job is set in motion through an intentional and unusual emphasis on the word "blessing," a word which first shows up as part of Job's concern for his children. The Hebrew word for "bless," *barach*, is used in two contrasting ways in the first two chapters of Job, sometimes straightforwardly as "bless," and sometimes as a euphemism for "curse." There is no simple explanation for this, other than the possibility that the word was either used colloquially—perhaps with a specific emphasis or tone—to refer to its opposite, or that it was used euphemistically to refrain from articulating the blasphemous idea of cursing God, a severe offense in ancient Israel. We can do something that is perhaps similar in modern English if we place a sarcastic emphasis on the word "thanks," turning it from a straightforward expression of gratitude (*"thank you!"*) to an implication of its opposite (*"thanks a lot..."*). Unfortunately, this nuance of the Hebrew language is difficult to capture in translation, and so the intentional repetition of the word "bless"—and the irony with which it is used—is often lost on the modern reader. Contrary to what one might think when reading most English translations, in the opening two chapters of Job the word "curse" never actually appears; it is always the word bless, and only the context tells us whether it means blessing or "blessing." The unusual and perhaps even playful emphasis on this ambiguity highlights blessing as an important theme for the audience.

The word bless is first used at the end of Job's introduction, in the context of Job's anxiety about his children and their inner thoughts toward God. Job's anxiety around the state of his children's inner disposition in blessing or "blessing" God helps transition the reader or listener into the next portion of the story, shifting from the introduction of Job to a series of heavenly council scenes which revolve around the idea of divine blessing and human response. Two distinct scenes follow one another in 1:6-22 and 2:1-10, each one moving from dialogue within the divine council to the subsequent events in Job's life. The portrayal of the divine council would have been familiar and easily recognizable to the original audience of the book of Job. It was a regular day in heaven, with God holding court with the heavenly beings, collectively referred to as the "sons of God," doing the business of running the universe. As the first divine council scene opens, we learn that a figure named Satan—a name which literally means "Adversary" or "Accuser," and who functions in the story through that role—shows up at the divine council and challenges God on the veracity of Job's faith:

One day, when the sons of God came to present themselves to the LORD, the Accuser also came in their midst. The LORD said to the Accuser, "Where have you come from?" The Accuser answered the LORD and said, "From roaming the earth, going this way and that." The LORD said to the Accuser, "Have you considered my servant Job? There is none like him on earth: living with integrity, a righteous man, fearing God and shunning evil."

Job 1:6-8

Like a proud parent, God wants to show off Job's righteousness and faithfulness, but the Accuser accuses Job, saying that it is only because of his prosperity and blessed life that Job is faithful to God:

The Accuser answered the LORD and said, "Does Job fear God without reason? Have you not put a fence around him, and his household, and everything around him? You have blessed the work of his hands, and his herds have spread out across the land; but stretch out your hand and strike all that he has, and see if he doesn't bless you to your face." The LORD said to the Accuser, "Look, all that he has is in your hand; only against him you will not stretch out your hand."

Job 1:9-11

If God were to take away the blessings of Job's life, the Accuser states, Job would respond by "blessing" God to God's face. Context makes it clear that the Accuser is really implying that Job will curse God to God's face, though Job's response makes the claim an ironic prediction of his faithfulness. After the first divine council scene, the perspective shifts back to earth, where Job learns of the destruction and theft of his property and the death of his household, along with the death of his ten children. The news is relayed by four messengers, continuing the theme of symbolic completeness from Job's introduction. However, in this instance, rather than completeness and harmony, it reflects the symbolic totality of the destruction of all that Job has. Each message ends with the haunting refrain: "*I alone have escaped to tell you.*"

Job's response to the destruction of his property and the death of his children is to bless God, demonstrating his commitment in words that have echoed throughout religious services and sentiments in history:

Naked I came from my mother's womb,
and naked I shall return there.
The LORD gave, and the LORD has taken away;
blessed be the name of the LORD.

Job 1:21

Job's response is expressed through poetry that is exquisite in its ability to convey complex layers of meaning in a few short lines. The first phrase is a straightforward one, witnessing to the truth that we all enter the world as naked infants; the second phrase transposes that image of birth to the reality of death, framing death as a return to the womb and the concept of clothing metaphorically as the possessions and relationships acquired throughout life. In *The Book of Job: A Contest of Moral Imaginations,* Carol Newsom captures the juxtaposition of poetic imagery well by writing that through Job's loss he has been "stripped of all that clothes a human life."[2] For Job, God's giving and taking away is framed by the boundaries of life and death, seen through the dominant image of birth and maternal love. Job proclaims that his existence in life and death is surrounded by God, the one who brought him into being and the one to whom he will return after death. Everything he has was given to him by God, and if God takes it away, then so be it—he accepts the loss and still chooses to bless God.

Immediately after the first divine council scene and the loss of Job's possessions, household, and children, there is a second divine council scene. The Accuser returns to the heavenly court, still unsatisfied with the veracity of Job's faith. After an introduction that parallels the first divine council scene, God renews the challenge to the Accuser concerning Job's faithfulness:

The LORD said to the Accuser, "Have you considered my servant Job? There is none like him on earth: living with integrity, a righteous man, fearing God and shunning evil. He continues in his integrity, even though you incited me to destroy him without reason." The Accuser answered the LORD and said, "Skin for skin! A man will give everything for his own life. Just stretch out your hand and strike his bone and his flesh, and see if he doesn't bless you to your face." The LORD said to the Accuser, "He is in your hand; but you will spare his life."

    Job 2:3-6

After the second divine council scene, Job is stricken with a painful disease, and sits outside the town walls on a pile of ashes, scraping at the sores on his skin with a piece of broken pottery. His wife, the only immediate family member left to him, speaks to him and says:

"Are you still continuing in your integrity? Bless God and die."
    Job 2:9b

Rather than receiving consolation from his wife, Job's pain is exacerbated by her words. His response to her, also serving indirectly as a response to the second divine council scene, is perhaps slightly more ambiguous than his first response, though still an expression of profound commitment to his religious convictions:

24

He said to her, "You speak as a fool speaks. Should we accept only the good things from God, and not the bad as well?"
Job 2:10a

If Job's first response provided a view of human life surrounded by God in maternal love and care, in which there are no guarantees for what is given or taken away, Job's second response articulates the belief that life itself is a bit of a mixed bag, with experiences that are both good and evil.

According to Job, our role as faithful humans is to accept either fortune or misfortune from God with equanimity. There is a sense, though, in which Job's second response contains subtle hints of dissonance. Job does not explicitly bless God in his second response, but neither does he "bless" God like the Accuser had predicted or his wife suggests. For those paying attention to the drama centered around the kind of blessing Job gives to God, the initial tension remains unresolved. God's initial blessing seems to have become instead a curse on Job's life. While Job has expressed his acceptance of what has happened to him, he has still not explicitly blessed God. Will he bless God? Or will he end up "blessing" God for the devastation of his life? How will Job ultimately respond to his test of faith?

By framing the heavenly council scenes and the events of Job's life in this way, the author draws the audience into the first major conceptual paradigm of the book: the idea that suffering and evil in this world are God-ordained tests of faith. In a reflection of Job's own insecurity and fear about what is truly in the hearts of his children, God's inability to know if Job is truly faithful causes God to attempt to reveal Job's inner character by bringing suffering and evil into his life. This drama of faith unfolds on a cosmic scale, framed as a contest between God and the Accuser, with Job's faithfulness on trial. It is a grand and sweeping story—but it is nonetheless part of the author's initial misdirection.

Brilliantly, the author begins the story by drawing the audience into a common and seemingly natural paradigm of interpretation. Most of us would be familiar with some version of the idea that God is up in heaven ordaining the events of the world; evil and suffering (carried out by the Accuser after securing divine permission as a representative of the forces of chaos and evil in the world) are actively permitted by God because they are needed to reveal either the veracity or hypocrisy of human faithfulness. The fact that God's motives seem to reflect Job's own worry for his children and the true state of their hearts makes the situation seem even more natural. If we are suffering, it is because God is testing us; it is because God needs to test our faith to make sure it does not depend on life's circumstances. This is a perspective that the author will systematically deconstruct in the first half of the book, following it with the reconstruction of something else entirely. While it is important to explore exactly what the author's purpose is in drawing the audience into this paradigm, the idea of suffering as a divine test of faith is not the only paradigm present in the first half of the book. There is also a second misdirection employed.

The theme of Job's test of faith and his "blessing" of God is left unresolved after the second divine council scene, and a new theme is introduced by Job's three friends, Eliphaz, Bildad, and Zophar, each of whom makes a lengthy journey to be with him in his suffering:

When they heard of all the evil that had come upon him, three of Job's friends came to him, each from their own place: Eliphaz the Temanite, Bildad the Shuhite, and Zophar the Naamathite. They joined together to come and grieve with him, and to console him. When they lifted up their eyes from afar, it was as if they did not know him; so they lifted up their voices and wept, and each one tore his robe, and threw dust into the air to cover his head. They sat with him on the earth for seven days and seven nights, and no one said a word to him, for they saw the depth of his suffering.
Job 2:11-13

The journey of the friends and the actions they take to grieve with Job continue the ongoing theme of numerical symbolism. Three prominent sages, each from a different land, come to see what comfort they can offer their friend Job when they hear of all the tragedy that has befallen him. Upon seeing him and being unable at first even to recognize him because of his affliction, they respond with a three-fold expression of grief: weeping, tearing their robes, and throwing dust onto their heads. After this, they sit with him in silence for seven days and seven nights, a complete week. These actions convey a wonderful sense of solidarity and presence; they are not superficial or glib but speak to the depth of their friendship with Job and their desire to care for him.

After those seven days and nights, however, a dialogue begins between Job and his three friends. That dialogue will be the focus of the next chapter, but it is possible at this point to outline the other major paradigm that the author of Job introduces through the perspective of Job's three friends. Their perspective is expressed as the idea that the events that comprise a person's life are all a form of divine retribution, whether for good or for ill, what scholars often refer to as the theory of retributive justice. The idea is that if a person does good, God blesses them; if they do evil, God brings down punishment on them. Looking at Job's situation from within this paradigm, since God clearly brought down severe punishment on Job, the only logical conclusion in the minds of Job's friends is that Job must have done something wrong. Whatever Job's action or inaction was, it is clear to the friends that Job needs to repent from whatever caused such a severe response of divine displeasure and turn to God in renewed faith.

The rationalizations of Job's friends are an attempt to explain the events of Job's life by discerning moral culpability through cause-and-effect reasoning. Implicit in their perspective is the idea that there needs to be a reason behind the events of Job's life. What caused these things to happen? Within their paradigm of understanding, a good and holy God would not permit such suffering to fall upon an innocent person. The only possible conclusion for the friends is that the blame lies with Job, who needs to come clean about his hidden wrongdoing and turn back to God in repentance and humility. While we might not articulate the case of God's retributive justice in the same way as Job's friends today, the impulse to rationalize suffering by trying to figure out who or what is to blame—often focused on the person or group who has actually experienced the suffering—is very much alive and well. It is a natural human response, but that does not mean it is true. Job's rejection of this so-called wisdom and the escalating conflict between him and his three friends comprise the rest of the first half of the book, all the way to the "end" of Job's words in chapter thirty-one.

The book of Job is not a theological treatise that advances an argument in logical steps. It is a piece of inspired literature, a creative work of art in which the author is actively shaping the story, intentionally engaging with the reader or listener. Two primary themes in the first half of the book frame Job's suffering through certain paradigms of interpretation: suffering as a test of faithfulness and suffering as retribution for sin or wrongdoing. The whole first half of the book is built on the drama and tension centered on these two themes. Will Job pass the test of faith and bless God, despite his immense suffering? Will the friends successfully reveal a secret sin in Job's life, or manage to figure out who or what is to blame? Or will they be able to convince Job that humanity is simply and fundamentally sinful, deserving of God's wrath, and that he should accept his just punishment and submit to God in order to experience restoration?

The brilliance of what the author is doing can be seen in the way the story identifies what are perhaps the two most common and most harmful ways to interpret suffering within a religious context: either "this is happening because someone (likely you) did something wrong" or "God is using this to test the strength and veracity of your faith." If Job were a theological treatise, the author could state those premises and then make an argument showing them to be false—but Job is not a theological treatise. Instead, the author crafts a narrative which begins with those very ideas and then systematically deconstructs them, following that deconstruction with an elegant reconstruction and bringing the reader or listener into a radical paradigm shift in the process. The initial premises of Job's story are systematically deconstructed, and a new paradigm of understanding is introduced as the book of Job builds to its climactic "aha!" moment in the revelation of God.

As the first half of the book unfolds, both paradigms for understanding suffering are brought into increasing cognitive dissonance on the part of the reader or listener. Descending into the depths of the valley of suffering with Job is not easy. As the book progresses toward chapter thirty-one and the "end" of Job's words, the tensions inherent in those initial paradigms of understanding build to a breaking point. Job voices all the problems and difficulties with those ways of thinking about suffering in a spirit of painful clarity. It is far more effective to deconstruct a view from within than it is to argue against it from without, and it is through identification with the character of Job—another literary device used to great effect—that the whole paradigm of suffering introduced in the first half of the book begins to fracture.

3

Dry rivers in a wasteland
Job 3-31

More than half of the book of Job is comprised of increasingly contentious poetic speeches spoken by Job and his three friends, Eliphaz, Bildad, and Zophar. Poetic speeches themselves, a highly valued form of artistic expression in cultures that emphasize the spoken word, can feel unfamiliar and intimidating to readers who are unaccustomed to them. From a literary perspective, though, there is an excellent reason for the length and form of this portion of the book. By taking the necessary time and space to draw the audience deeply into the pain and suffering of Job, the author causes the readers or listeners of the story to identify deeply with him. This identification is strengthened by the first-person form of the speeches, which gives them a sense of immediacy, as if the audience were actually present and listening to the words being spoken. Rather than being told about Job, we are invited to share in his pain through his agonized speeches and impassioned accusations:

Oh, if only my anguish could be weighed,
all my ruin heaped on a scale!
It would surely outweigh the sand in the sea—
thus my reckless words!
     Job 6:2-3

Through these speeches, Job becomes more than a name on a page; Job becomes a person, a character who elicits our compassion and challenges our assumptions. It is easy to hold certain ideas about suffering as long as it is kept at an appropriate distance. It is when we experience suffering ourselves, though, or can identify with someone who has suffered deeply, that the supposed wisdom of superficial religiosity and its easy answers begin to unravel. Job begins by explicitly cursing his own life and expressing his grief in an honest and extreme way:

Job opened his mouth and cursed his day:

"Damn the day of my birth,[3]
the night that said, 'A man is conceived!'

That day—
     let it become darkness
     let God above not seek it

let no light shine on it
let darkness and death-shadow claim it
let a fog settle on it
let terror eclipse that day.

That night—
  let shadows seize it
  let it not appear with the days of the year
  let it not come into the count of moons
oh, that night—
  let it be barren
  let no joyful cry come to it
  let the day-cursers curse it
  those ready to expose Leviathan
  let its evening stars grow dark
  let it wait for light and—
      nothing
  let it never see the eyelids of the dawn."
      Job 3:1-9

Job's lament contrasts with his prior responses to his suffering. After the loss of his children, household, and possessions, his first response connected the idea of birth with God's act of giving and taking away, using the womb as an image for both life

35

and death. Job now takes that same image of birth and moves it in a new direction. The horizons of God's maternal care that encompass human life morph into a horrific and oppressive reality, surrounded by a God who seems distant and cruel. Rather than either blessing or "blessing" God, Job curses the day of his birth and the night of his conception. Day and night are paired together in a striking poetic twist to encompass the entirety of his own creation as a human being. In his lament, Job is not simply wishing that he had never been born, and he is not only expressing grief so profound that he actively longs for death; in his lament, Job curses God's very act of creation in making and sustaining him. The foundational dimensions of creation—day and night, light and darkness, an orderly progression of time, the act of conception, and the birth of new life—all fall under Job's curse in chapter three as he wishes for darkness, death, and chaos to wash over his world and unmake it. Job cries out:

Why did I not perish in the womb,
expire during birth?
Why did knees greet me,
why breasts, that I might nurse?
　　　Job 3:11-12

Job wishes that he had died in the womb, that there had been no family or community to receive him or care for him, and he expresses a longing for a swift path to death, the only place he can imagine finding rest and peace. He concludes his lament by connecting his pain to eating and drinking, the basic actions that sustain life:

Groans have replaced my food
my lament is like water poured out
what I dreaded is here
what I feared has arrived
>   *I have no ease—*
>   *I have no quiet—*
>   *I have no rest—*
>   *torment has come.*
>   Job 3:24-26

Job's lament is filled with disquieting poetic images centered on darkness and death, often introducing a theme like infancy or joy and then altering it to something death-dealing or distorted to reflect the kind of reversal he has experienced in life. The compassionate presence of Eliphaz, Bildad, and Zophar and their willingness to sit with Job in his anguish create the necessary space for Job to express his deep suffering. How he does so, through poetry, is both a part of the artistry of the book and a witness to its practical wisdom. Suffering is portrayed in a manner that speaks to the human experience, finding its voice in the context of loving support from a committed community and taking form through vivid creative expression.

The sense of community and support from Job's friends begins to fall apart, though, the moment the friends break their silence and offer Job their "wisdom." Eliphaz, Bildad, and Zophar try to console Job by framing his life and experiences within a particular religious paradigm of sin and repentance. They seem to consider this a helpful response, since by framing Job's experience in this manner they can situate Job in the middle of a coherent narrative, one that explains why his suffering occurred and which also provides a path to a happy ending through the renewal of Job's life. Carol Newsom articulates an importantly nuanced point about the friends' response to Job by saying that the friends are seeking to "restore to Job a sense of narrative, or more fundamentally, a sense of the narratability of his life."[4] Eliphaz's first speech, which is also the first response of the friends to Job's lament, outlines a general temporal progression as he traces out the basic plot he sees unfolding in Job's life. He begins by establishing common ground, appealing to the advice which Job has given to others in the past:

Look! You have admonished many
and restored feeble hands to strength;
your words have made stumblers firm,
those sinking to their knees you have strengthened.
   Job 4:3-4

Eliphaz claims that Job has habitually acted as an upright man who supported others in their trials through words of wisdom and consolation. Now, however, Job has been struck by terrible calamity himself, and has lost sight of his own wisdom and perspective:

But now it comes upon you,
and you are sorely tried;
it strikes you,
and you are dismayed.
   Job 4:5

From the viewpoint of his friends, Job needs the same consolation he has faithfully offered to so many. He is simply distraught because of the intensity of his suffering, and needs to be reminded of some basic truths about God and how the world functions:

39

Is not your reverence your confidence?
Your hope the integrity of your ways?
Recall—what righteous person has perished?
Where have the upright been cut off?
This is what I have seen:
>*those who plow iniquity,*
>*those who sow trouble,*
>*they are the ones who harvest it.*
>   Job 4:6-8

Through these words, Eliphaz expresses the basic outline of retributive justice. Good works are rewarded in kind; evil is paid back in full. According to this perspective, Job's suffering is interpreted as retribution for sin. At this point in his speech, Eliphaz throws in a subtle twist, which he backs up by appealing to his own spiritual experiences. He suggests that in Job's case, his sin could have been unintentional, or perhaps an unfortunate instance of simply being a pervasively sinful human being trying to measure up to the holiness of the divine:

A word was carried to me—
my ear caught the slightest whisper;
in visions of the night,
when sleep falls on humankind,

fear and trembling came upon me;
all my bones shook.
A spirit passed before me—
the hair on my flesh shivered;
it stood still, but I could not perceive its form.
An image confronted my eyes,
in the stillness I heard a voice:

"Can a person be righteous before God?
Can a man be pure before his maker?"
         Job 4:12-17

Eliphaz's own spiritual experiences concerning the difference between sinful humanity and a holy God are used to explain the discrepancy between Job's experience of suffering and his apparent life of righteousness. According to Eliphaz, Job may not even know where he went wrong. Perhaps being human is simply enough to condemn a person before God. Instead of being dismayed and discouraged by this reality, however, Job should appeal to God, who is able to bring about transformation and healing. Ultimately, according to Eliphaz, what Job needs to do is to accept his suffering as part of God's discipline, knowing that no one is truly righteous before God, and turn to God so that he can live into renewed abundance:

Look—happy is the man whom God rebukes!
Do not despise the Almighty's discipline.
He injures, but he binds up,
he shatters, but his hands heal.

Look—all this we have searched,
> *so hear it,*
> *and apply it to yourself.*
Job 5:17-18, 27

In his speech, Eliphaz provides what he thinks is a plausible explanation for why Job suffered, and also what Job should do to be restored to the fullness of life. He expects his wisdom to be a balm to Job, helpful in restoring him to his previous state of faith and prosperity. Job's response, though, is one of anger and vehement rejection. He is unwilling to accept the religious paradigm expressed by Eliphaz as he wrestles through the lived experience of his suffering, an experience which has opened his eyes to the reality of a world that does not correspond to Eliphaz's simplistic narrative. While Eliphaz is trying to situate Job within a paradigmatic and coherent tale of sin and reconciliation, Job chooses to remain in the present fragmented reality of his suffering. Job is unwilling to sit passively and accept whatever comes his way as though it were some piece of God's larger plan, or as somehow reflective of God's higher righteousness, inaccessible and incomprehensible to mere mortals. Job wants an answer, and he is willing to challenge the status quo to receive it. His radical truth-telling exposes the ultimately callous and unsatisfying nature of the theological perspective of his friends.

As the speeches progress, an overall sense of symmetry and directionality emerges. The progression of speakers follows the general pattern Eliphaz – Job – Bildad – Job – Zophar – Job. This happens three times, with each of the friends giving three speeches, until the final cycle of speeches where Bildad only gets in a few lines and Zophar is completely silent. The tone of the friends gets more and more heated and confrontational in trying to accuse Job of explicit sin, until finally in the third and final round the friends' speeches sputter out. Eliphaz makes one last attempt to convince Job, where he confronts him directly with accusations of injustice and cruelty, Bildad gives the shortest speech of the series, and Zophar makes no comment at all. Scholars have often sought to "find" a third speech for Zophar or have rearranged the text to add material to Bildad's final speech, but this cut-and-paste approach ignores the symbolic nature of the descent into silence and fractured confusion on the part of the friends. The friends' confusion and increasingly accusatory tone are set in contrast to Job, who continues to develop his line of thought as the book progresses. Compositionally, this conveys the distinct sense that the friends have less and less of an answer for Job, a fact that they seek to cover up by an increasingly combative posture. Their wisdom is being reduced to angry silence in the face of Job's defense.

Job never claims sinlessness for himself while arguing with his friends about the reason behind his experience of suffering. He simply points out that his experience of suffering extends far beyond any sort of proportionate retribution or divine discipline. If it is true that God has brought this suffering down upon him for some wrong or sin in his life, then God is an unjust judge, meting out punishment disproportionate to the crime. Job has experienced profound suffering, something which has opened his eyes not only to his own suffering but also to the suffering and oppression of others in the world, all the poor and marginalized people who suffer daily under the power of the unjust. That reality gives him a picture of a God who seems blatantly cruel and distant. In poetic verse evocative of fragmented, anguished expression, Job reflects on his innocence, saying:

Blameless, I—
I know not myself;
I reject my life.
It's all one—so I say
he destroys both blameless and wicked.

If death lashes suddenly
he mocks the despair of the innocent.
   Job 9:21-23

Job's accusation of God here is merely one example of what enrages his friends—he claims that God actively mocks the sudden death of the innocent. Job is not willing to accept the narrative of the friends about divine discipline and repentance. He points out all the instances of wrongdoing and suffering in the world that appear to go unanswered by God, situations that seem to reflect a God who is absent, or perhaps even actively in support of evildoers:

My very soul loathes my life—
  I will set loose my complaint,
  I will speak from the bitter places of my soul.
I say to God,
  "Do not condemn me—
  show me why you contend with me!
  Is it somehow good, when you oppress?
  When you reject the work of your hand,
  and shine on the purposes of the wicked?"
   Job 10:1-3

Job also questions his friends, challenging their superficial view of the world and the supposedly straightforward fate of both righteous and evildoers:

Look! I know your thoughts,
the plots by which you would wrong me.
You would say:
>*"Where now is the house of the nobles?*
>*Where is the tent, the dwelling-place of the wicked?"*
Have you not asked those who travel the roads?
Do you not know by their markings?
>*In the day of disaster, the wicked are preserved;*
>*in the day of overflowing wrath,*
>*they are carried to safety.*
>
>   Job 21:27-30

Job's claims are a direct challenge to the wisdom of his friends. He is looking at the world with eyes tinted by his own experience of suffering, and what he sees is a world where the wicked prosper and the righteous suffer. This pattern of struggle, not so much with the existence of God as with the nature of who God is, resonates with the struggles of others. C.S. Lewis, in *A Grief Observed*, a book in which he reflects on his sorrow and grief after the death of his wife, writes: "not that I am (I think) in much danger of ceasing to believe in God. The real danger is of coming to believe such dreadful things about Him. The conclusion I dread is not 'So there's no God after all,' but 'So this is what God's really like. Deceive yourself no longer.'"[5]

Job consistently rejects the paradigm offered by his three friends. He is not interested in their wisdom and is wounded by what it implies in his case. The friends, for their part, are not interested in listening to Job or hearing the dissonant perspective that Job is developing. In pursuing their line of argument, they end up expressing things that are downright cruel. The blatant callousness of their accusations serves to bring their paradigm of understanding into increasing tension for the reader or listener. Bildad, for example, opens his first speech by indicting Job's sons, thoughtless words spoken to a bereaved father grieving for lost children:

How long will you speak like this,
a mighty wind spewing from your mouth?
Does God turn judgment crooked?
Does the Almighty bend justice?
If your sons sinned against him,
he sent them on for their transgressions.
        Job 8:2-4

Zophar, for his part, seems to imply in his first speech that Job's physical disfigurement is due to his moral failure, saying:

If you would make firm your heart,
and spread your palms to him;
If you would remove iniquity from your hand,
and let no injustice dwell in your tent,
surely then you would lift up your face, without blemish!
You would become firm, and without fear,
for you would forget your anguish,
the memory of it like waters flowing by.
        Job 11:14-16

The implication of Zophar's words about Job's blemished face overshadows the beautiful image of suffering as a river in motion, the experience soon downstream with life-refreshing restoration still flowing by. It is no wonder that Job responds to comments like these in anger and anguish, comparing his friends to dry rivers in a wasteland. They came to him, full of promised snowmelt from a far land, and yet were discovered to be dry upon arrival, a catastrophic situation for a thirsty traveler:

My brothers are like a faithless desert stream,
like a stream that flows across lands,
dark under the ice, flush with snowmelt,
        but when the dry season comes, they vanish—
        in the heat they leave their place

turn aside their wandering path
ascend into trackless waste
and are lost.
Job 6:15-18

In addition to continuing to witness to his innocence against his friends' accusations, refusing to enter into the narrative of suffering as retribution for sin of some kind, Job also begins to use explicitly legal language, articulating a formal case against God. Job wants to contend with God in a legal context to establish his uprightness in contrast to his friends' accusations, and to hear what reason God would possibly have for bringing so much pain and suffering into his life. Job's legal case develops slowly over his speeches. In response to Bildad's first speech, Job challenges the idea of God's justice on the grounds of being unable to genuinely interact with God or make a case for his own innocence:

Truly, I know this is so,
but how can a person defend their righteousness to God?

Even if I called, and he answered,
I do not know that he would listen to my voice.
He would crush me with a whirlwind,
and multiply my wounds without reason.
Job 9:2, 16-17

Job's image of being crushed by a divine whirlwind foreshadows the book's climax, though God when revealed turns out to be quite different from what Job pictures at this point. Job advances this theme in his next speech by asking God to lay out the case against him and make it clear where he went wrong:

Call, and I will answer—
or I will speak, and you respond:
what are my iniquities and my sins?
Teach me my sin and my transgression!
   Job 13:22-23

Job's case rests on the idea that he has done nothing to deserve the suffering he has experienced, and that God has wronged him by inexplicably turning on him and bringing destruction down on his life. To Job, it seems as though God, who used to be his friend, has betrayed him, as though God has broken faith with him. Job's case is striking in its brutal honesty and willingness to speak truth from his own perspective, even if that means accusing God of wrong. In different parts of his speeches, Job gives voice to the perception of God as his enemy:

He hates me and tears at me in anger,
gnashing his teeth,
my opponent sharpens his gaze on me.

I was at ease, but he shattered me,
he seized me by the neck and threw me;
he made me a target,
and surrounded me with archers;
he pierces my kidneys,
no mercy;
he spills my bile on the earth.

I yell "Violence!"
No one answers.
I cry out, and there is no justice.
He has walled off my path,
I cannot pass;
darkness is set on my road.
He has stripped me of glory,
he has torn the crown from my head,
he tears me down on every side
          I am gone—
my hope uprooted like a tree.
          Job 16:9, 12-14; 19:7-10

In contrast to Job's three friends, who tend to speak only to Job in their speeches, perhaps refusing to address God out of a sense of piety, Job addresses his complaint to God directly. In the midst of this overwhelming anguish, Job cries out for relief:

Why did you draw me out of the womb?
Oh, that I had perished there
with no eye to see me;
my life would have been a non-existence,
a straight path from womb to grave.
Are not my days few?
Cease, please! Leave me alone—
that I might take what little happiness is left me,
before I leave for the land of no return,
of darkness and death-shadow;
> *a land as dark as blackest night,*
> *a land of chaos*
> *where even the light is darkness.*
>> Job 10:18-22

These shocking portrayals of God's character and brutal descriptions of Job's suffering are all a part of the case he builds against God, which receives its final articulation after the friends have ceased to argue with Job. Job's dialogue with Eliphaz,

Bildad, and Zophar ends after the third cycle of speeches, with Job then making his formal case against God in chapters twenty-nine through thirty-one. In his case against God, Job is trying to chart a new course that moves past the limited narrative and perspective of the friends about sin and suffering. His experience does not fit into their paradigm of suffering as a result of sin or as divine discipline of some kind, and he is not satisfied with receiving a superficial theological explanation from his friends for his suffering. Job doesn't want an answer from his three friends; he wants an answer from God.

Job begins his case against God in chapter twenty-nine by reflecting on his life, witnessing to his state of blamelessness:

When the ear heard—it commended me;
when the eye saw—it sought to emulate me;
because I delivered the afflicted who cried for help,
the orphan, and the one who had nowhere to turn.
The blessing of the perishing came to me,
I was the cause of widows rejoicing.
Righteousness I wore as my clothing,
justice was my robe and turban,
eyes for the blind, and feet for the lame—that was I.
　　　Job 29:11-15

Job lays the groundwork for his case by constructing a moral framework of sorts that corresponds to the traditional social world he inhabited. As Job's speech unfolds in chapters twenty-nine and thirty, the social world spreads out around him in larger and larger concentric circles: his family, the respected men and leaders of his town, the needy and marginalized whom he aids, the larger social community, and finally the outcasts, exiles who live in the wilderness. Job claims that he lived as a righteous person, a patron and an advocate for the marginalized and oppressed, someone who held a position of honor and esteem in his community. Now, however, he has been turned into an outcast, mocked and persecuted even by those who are themselves exiled from society. He has been cast from the center of his social world to the margins.

After describing his social turmoil and dislocation, Job focuses on the reason for his suffering: God's apparent faithlessness to him. God is described as merciless in a way that Job would never even consider, ignoring the cry of an afflicted person and even going so far as to add to their distress:

Surely no one stretches out a hand against a ruin,
if that ruin were to cry out for help?
Have I not wept for those in a time of hardship?
Has my soul not grieved for the poor?
    I looked for good—but evil came.

I waited for light—then came darkness.
Job 30:24-26

In his case against God, Job situates himself as one of the needy, unjustly cast to the margins of his social world, and he seeks restoration from God. Job claims to have lived as a benevolent patron in society, caring for those who suffered calamity and misfortune, and he calls on God to do so as well. Job imagines God as the ideal judge and social exemplar, the one who will hear his case and respond with mercy and compassion. God should hear Job's case and respond as Job himself would to someone wrongly accused and in need. According to the social and moral framework laid out by Job, God must step in to confront the wicked and care for the needy. If God refuses to do so, then the implicit conclusion is that God must be unjust, or at least less just than Job.

Chapter thirty-one, the final piece of Job's case and the end of the first half of the book, is comprised of a long oath which Job swears to seal his legal case as he seeks vindication. Legally speaking, Job is witnessing to his innocence in the strongest way possible, calling down God's wrath on himself should he be found false. Job's oath is made up of a series of many potential sins, where Job first articulates the possibility of doing something wrong and then pronounces divine judgment on himself if it should be found to be true:

If I have stepped off the path,
if my eyes have led my heart,
if any blemish clings to my hand—
> *then let me sow, and another eat,*
> *let the fruit of my labor be uprooted.*

If I have seen someone perishing for lack of clothing,
or a poor man without a garment;
if he did not bless me,
warmed by my sheep's fleece;
if I have raised my hand against the orphan,
enabled by my influence at the town gate—
> *then let my shoulder be pulled out of joint,*
> *let the bone of my arm be shattered.*
> Job 31:7-8, 19-22

If Job has acted wickedly, he lays out proportional punishment for himself; if he is innocent, however, his innocence must be acknowledged as well. What Job is doing through his oath and case against God is subtle but powerful. The suffering he has experienced and the silence of God in failing to respond either to it or to him permitted his friends to assume Job's guilt before God. According to the friends, if Job were genuinely righteous, God would never have brought this calamity upon him. By making his case against God and swearing this oath, however, Job has turned the tables on the silence of God and the arguments put forward by his friends. Rather than the burden of proof lying with Job in proving his innocence, the burden of proof is now on God either to show where Job is guilty, or to admit wrongdoing in bringing undeserved suffering into Job's life. Moreover, Job has made his case directly to God through a binding legal oath. Job's friends no longer have recourse to their theological arguments but must stand by the action or inaction of God in either punishing or providing restitution for Job.

As Job draws his case to its conclusion in the culmination of the first half of the book, the author of Job has drawn us as readers and listeners into a state of profound dissonance. In the opening scenes of the story, it was Job's character that was on the line, Job's faith that was questioned by the Accuser, Job's response of blessing or "blessing" that the audience was waiting expectantly for. Through his radical honesty, Job not only dismantles the simplistic religious narrative of sin and repentance expressed by his friends, but also turns his initial test of faith back on God—it is now God's character that is in question, God's apparent injustice, and God's lack of faithfulness to Job. Job's claim of injustice and his legal case against God have a discomforting ring of truthfulness to them. They have a sincerity that silences Job's friends, and they drive Job to go toe-to toe with God, not in cynical rejection but in honest and agonized challenge. As Job draws his final speech to a close, just before the "end" of his words in 31:40, he stands defiant before God, saying:

Here is my signature—let the Almighty answer,
let my opponent put it in writing!
> *I would carry it on my shoulder,*
> *I would bind it on my head like a crown,*
> *I would declare my every step to him,*
> *I would approach him like a prince!*
> Job 31:35b-37

Just after this challenge, Job's words are declared by the author to be ended. The word "end" used to describe Job's words in 31:40, *tamam*, is the same root word used in Job's introduction at the beginning of the book to describe Job as a person with integrity. It is a word that conveys the completeness, wholeness, or fullness of something, and it serves as a fitting symbolic *inclusio* for the first half of the book. When the story began, Job was described as a complete person, living what would have been thought of as the fullness of human life. He then experienced a symbolically complete tragedy, losing virtually everything in his life. After the arrival of his three friends, Job expressed his grief honestly and completely, ultimately weaving it together into a final case against God. At this point, his words—his grief and the honest expression of his pain and anger—are "full," they are "complete," with nothing left to add. Job has said his piece; his words are ended. The finality with which Job's words are said to be finished gives a sense that the story is over, that he has suffered and expressed everything, and that there is nothing left for his friends to say or do.

It is perhaps no wonder, then, that the scene at the end of the first half of the book is one of fractured silence. Job has rebuffed the so-called wisdom offered by his friends and thrown a potentially blasphemous challenge at God, refusing to bend his knee in false piety to an unjust God who would break faith with him. This is not a comfortable place to be for anyone who wants to maintain a sense of faith in God or God's goodness, and as Job's final words fade, the silence weighs thick all around. According to Job, it is not him who needs to address his wrongdoing—it is God. This is the lowest and darkest point of the story, where Job sits in an angry silence on an ash-heap, surrounded by his friends. His words are finished. But the "end" of Job's words is not the end of the story; in the silence it is possible to detect the slightest hint of a breeze beginning to stir. Job has made his case and spoken his words, all the way to the bitter end. Now it is time for someone else to step in and disrupt the story.

Part Two:
A Thunderstorm

4

Wisdom divided: above and below
Job 28

There is no interlude between the two halves of the book, no break between the end of Job's words and what comes next. Between the end of Job's dialogue with his friends and his final case against God, though, there is a chapter-long poem about the search for wisdom. It will be helpful to return to that wisdom poem in chapter twenty-eight before continuing because it lays a crucial thematic foundation for the second half of the book. From a compositional standpoint, the poem about wisdom also serves an important function by ending the dialogues between Job and his friends and creating a brief pause before Job begins his formal case against God, giving the audience a respite before plunging into his final lengthy speech and the shift into the second half of the book.

The poem speaks of searching for wisdom, describing the ways human beings have delved into the deep places of the earth to seek it. Mining is one of the metaphors used in the poem to portray the search for wisdom, one which speaks to the futility of human or earthly wisdom, wisdom that literally comes from the earth:

Surely there is a source for silver,
a place where gold is refined;
iron is taken from the earth,
copper smelted from ore.
They cut into the darkness, down to every end,
searching for precious stones
in darkness and death-shadow;

> *a shaft is broken open away from dwellings*
> *in a place untrodden by human feet;*
> *lowered down, they sway to and fro.*
> *From the earth comes forth bread,*
> *but underneath it is churned as by fire,*
> *it is the place of sapphires,*
> *precious stones and gold dust.*
> Job 28:1-6

Humans have tunneled deep into the earth to search out hidden things, carving open solid rock to bring precious stones and gems to the surface. When it comes to wisdom, though, the poem expresses that the search for such treasure is a futile one:

But wisdom—where can it be found?
Where is the place of understanding?
> Job 28:12

As the poem expresses, the deep recesses of the earth do not contain the wisdom Job needs; the sea confesses that wisdom is not to be found in it; there is no price, no amount of treasure that can be used to purchase wisdom; the wisdom that Job needs is found with God, and God alone. Wisdom from below, drawn up from the depths, is not enough, just as the wisdom of Job's friends proved empty.

If the first thirty-one chapters of Job show the futility of earthly wisdom, the following eleven chapters of the book are a reconstruction of something else, as Job's silence is broken by an unexpected voice. The second half of the book contains a detailed rearticulation of each aspect of the story that has come so far, but in a manner that is utterly transformed. There are speeches from a friend that help and redirect, rather than blame and harm, and an encounter with God that is astounding and utterly different from the kind of test of faith seen at the beginning of Job. In the first half of the story, we as readers and listeners walked alongside Job down into the valley of his suffering, all the way to the bottom, seeking earthly wisdom that would provide an adequate answer for Job's suffering. With the imagery of mining into the hidden places of the earth and searching out the depths of the sea, that earthly wisdom has reached its thematic completion and come up empty. Now, in the second half of the book, Job will be led up the other side of the valley, in what is described as God drawing Job into something new:

"He is wooing you from the jaws of distress,
to a spacious place free from restriction."
Job 36:16a (NIV)

If the first half of the book follows the trajectory of earthly, human wisdom, the second half is comprised of wisdom from above, wisdom revealed not by human seeking but from the very breath or spirit of God. Plumbing the depths of the earth and the sea turned up no answers, but the story is not yet finished. In the distance, barely discernable but slowly building in strength, tempestuous winds smash and whirl, lightning flickering in the roar of something powerful, something wild and uncontrollable—the imagery of a whirlwind from heaven, wisdom from above.

5

Wooed from the jaws of distress

Job 32-37

After the "end" of Job's words in chapter thirty-one, someone unexpected breaks the silence, someone who has until now been so far from center stage that he has been rendered essentially invisible. Elihu, son of Barakel—whose name means "he is my God," the son of "God blesses"—gets angry with Job and his friends. The Hebrew idiom is more literally translated "his nostrils were inflamed," a visceral description of anger. Elihu's brief introduction in 32:1-5 mentions anger four separate times. Elihu is angry at Job for his self-justification in the case he makes against God, and he is angry with the three friends because they proved to have no answer for Job. Inflamed nostrils serve to open and close Elihu's introduction, the burning anger of a zealous man. In the context of the story, however, this anger is not an improper response, nor is it the overreaction of an impetuous youth. In Elihu's speeches his anger is an expression of how much he cares for Job, and a witness to his firm grasp of who God really is.

Anger is not always perceived this way, and it may be difficult to see Elihu's anger as an expression of care. There is a scene in Fyodor Dostoevsky's famous novel *The Brothers Karamazov* where Ivan, the middle of the three brothers, explains to his younger brother Alyosha why he does not choose to profess faith in God. Ivan says that because of the suffering he has witnessed in the world, faith comes at a cost of intellectual honesty that he is unwilling to pay. In a speech reminiscent of Job's words, he describes the horrors experienced by innocent children in excruciating detail, saying that some vague promise of future redemption or hidden divine plan is not good enough for him. Ivan says: "I want to remain with unrequited suffering. I'd rather remain with my unrequited suffering and unquenched indignation, even if I am wrong.... It's not that I don't accept God, Alyosha, I just most respectfully return him the ticket."[6] In the midst of such suffering Alyosha's response is to give his brother a kiss, the answer of compassionate love in response to the profound evil of this world. The scene is famous for good reason and profound in its wisdom, but it is not the answer given by Job's friend Elihu. Elihu portrays another aspect of love, that of fiery indignation and challenge, witnessing to the errors of Job and the true character of God.

From a literary standpoint, Elihu serves a vital role in transitioning from Job's silence to the divine speeches in the book's final chapters. With all of our cultural differences, it is likely difficult for us today to see just how unexpected Elihu's interruption of the story is. He is a younger man rebuking his elders and presuming to instruct them—something which would have been a shocking breach of social protocol in Job's time. Because of this, his speeches begin with a defense of sorts, given to justify his presumption in speaking, where he remarks that it is not age or length of days that bestows true wisdom on a person, but rather the spirit of God:

Elihu son of Barakel the Buzite answered, saying:

"I am few in years, and you are aged,
so I withdrew in reverence,
not presuming to teach you.
I said, 'those with many days should speak,
those with an abundance of years should teach wisdom.'
But surely it is the spirit in a person,
the breath of the Almighty, that gives discernment."
Job 32:6-8

What Elihu seeks to offer is not wisdom from below, but from above. The beginning of this shift from human to divine highlights the foundational contrast between the two halves of the book. Elihu begins to chart a new path, bypassing the futility of human-based wisdom and giving voice to the true character and nature of God.

Elihu is no less direct in his confrontation with Job than the other three friends were. One of the key differences with Elihu is that he looks to witness to the truth about God rather than to accuse Job. Also, unlike the other friends, he actually responds to the claims he hears Job make, showing that he has listened carefully to what Job has been saying. Each of his speeches summarizes something that Job has expressed or implied, followed by Elihu contrasting that with the truth about who God is. Job's case is incredibly self-centered—*his* pain, *his* innocence, the injustice of God against *him*, the wrongs done to *him*. Rather than starting with Job and Job's case against God, Elihu begins with God and who God is. In contrast to the three cycles of speeches of Eliphaz, Bildad, and Zophar, Elihu's discourse is given in four parts. Being the fourth friend, there is a symbolic sense of completeness and wholeness to his speeches which transcends the wisdom of the other three friends, particularly with the way his fourth speech transitions seamlessly into God's self-revelation.

Elihu responds directly to Job, not to make him fearful or push him further down into his suffering and pain, but to challenge his errors and declare to him the truth about who God is. Job's first error is described in 33:8-11 as the claim that although he has lived a pure and upright life, God has become his enemy, chasing him down on every path in order to punish him. Job also claims that God does not speak to humans, and that he despairs of ever receiving an answer for his pain and suffering. Elihu's response, after declaring emphatically that God does speak to humanity (a reality made evident in an astounding way at the end of the book), points out that if someone is suffering the consequences of their sinful behavior, God's desire is not to punish them but to deliver them from that suffering, to bring them back to the fullness of life:

For God does speak—in one way, or another,
though no one notices;
in a vision in the night, a dream,
when sleep falls on people
and they slumber on their beds,
he uncovers their ears and opens instruction
to turn a person from acting
or to keep a mighty one from pride;
to restrain them from the pit,
their life from passing on in violence.
　　　Job 33:14-18

Along with these often-unnoticed nudges from God to restrain people from pursuing evil, Elihu also mentions the role of a mediator, someone who can stand between God and a person afflicted by their sins and destructive choices to intercede for them, to teach them how to act rightly, and to pray for them:

That person will pray to God for them
and God will accept them—
they will see God's face and give a joyful shout!
God will make a person's way right again.
      Job 33:26a

Through that mediator, the afflicted one can be restored to the fullness of life. Elihu states that God works, either directly through dreams and subtle nudges or indirectly through a mediator, to deliver and save from destruction and death. Sometimes Elihu's first speech is interpreted as saying that God uses suffering to teach people and to turn them away from sin, but the primary emphasis in Elihu's first speech is clearly on what God does for people either when they are afflicted by suffering or when they are about to make destructive decisions. Elihu never says that God brings suffering to people to teach them or turn them away from sin. He expresses that God's desire for people is:

To bring them back from the pit
so they might become bright with the light of life.
      Job 33:30

Sometimes that process happens through God's subtle warnings against doing evil, or sometimes through a mediator who illuminates what kind of sin or wrong action has led to a person's sickness or suffering, a person who is also able to restore that person to health and fullness of life. Job has claimed that God has betrayed him and become his enemy, but Elihu is adamant in his opposition to this idea. According to Elihu, God seeks redemption and restoration, and works to turn people away from wrongdoing—that is simply who God is.

Elihu next summarizes in 34:5-9 Job's claim that although he is innocent, God has denied him justice, and that there is no point in trying to please God. To this, Elihu's response is simple. God does not do evil, nor does God pervert justice. God acts with justice in governing this world, casting down evildoers and lifting up the oppressed:

For his eyes are on the paths of humankind,
all their steps he perceives.
There is no darkness, no death-shadow,
where doers of iniquity can hide.
There is no need for further consideration
or to go before him for judgment—
he breaks the mighty without inquiry
and sets others in their place.

Job 34:21-24

73

Elihu's view of God is not simplistic but balanced and nuanced. Although God desires and seeks restoration and healing, as Elihu made clear in his first speech, that emphasis does not mean that God refrains from enacting justice and overthrowing wickedness. God is just and righteous, and God acts with justice and righteousness—that is simply who God is. God knows every person and deed and acts accordingly.

According to Elihu, Job has gotten it wrong. God has not denied him justice. Job's image of God watching him expectantly, waiting for him to make a single mistake in order to punish him, is a distorted one. What is more, the difference between living in a way that is pleasing to God and a way that is evil, oppressive, and death-dealing, is radically important. Elihu witnesses to the character and truth of who God is, as though he is working to straighten out Job's distorted image of God. Although Elihu's words are close to those of Job's other friends when it comes to their perspective on God's justice, he doesn't use the idea of God's retribution to make the same argument as the friends by seeking to tie God to some human standard of retribution for good or evil. For Elihu, God is righteous, majestic, powerful, merciful, and good, but not in a simplistic or reducible kind of way, a perspective that is made clear in Elihu's third speech.

Elihu's third speech focuses on another of Job's claims, summarized in 35:1-2, that he gains nothing by keeping himself from wrongdoing. According to Job, God punishes him equally for his righteousness and his sin. Job claimed that he could have lived his life doing whatever he wanted, paying no attention to possible retribution from a capricious and inconsistent divinity. In response, Elihu rejects Job's underlying framework for interaction with God. Job spoke from the assumption that his sin harms God, and—as a logical corollary—that his righteousness benefits God. Once again, Elihu points out the falsehood behind Job's accusation. God is holy and is angered by sin, hurt by a humanity that turns away to their own destruction and the destruction of others, but God is not some universal balance sheet weighing out good and evil to determine someone's fate. God is angered by sin not because it harms God, but because it harms others, distorting and destroying humanity and the earth they live upon. Job is wrong when speaking about God's dealing with sin because God does not work by a simplistic principle of retributive justice:

Look to the heavens and consider:
take a moment to watch the clouds
as they float high above you.
If you sin—what is that to him?
If your transgressions are many—what does that do to him?
If you are righteous—what do you give to him?
*   What does he take from your hand?*

Your wickedness is done to a man like yourself,
your righteousness to another person.
　　　Job 35:5-8

God is just, and works justice, but not in the simplistic manner assumed by Job or his three friends. God does not act in a way driven by human action, whether good or bad. Job has things completely backwards, thinking that human sin or righteousness is what causes God to act. God is the one who acts with complete freedom, who initiates justice and brings it to fruition, who overthrows sin and extends the possibility of reconciliation. In this speech, Elihu offers a helpful corrective to the simplistic theology of Job's other friends. Eliphaz, Bildad, and Zophar took an idea that on the surface might seem plausible: God punishes the wicked and blesses the righteous. But in their arguments against Job, they misapplied that idea, assuming that human action is what drives God's response. As Job's life makes evident, sometimes the righteous suffer and the wicked prosper. The proper response to that reality is not to fit the world into a religious paradigm of retributive justice, but to embrace the freedom of a God who does act in bringing about both justice and restoration, though not in a way that is driven by human righteousness or sin.

　　Elihu's fourth speech is his longest, and transitions directly into God's own words. Elihu begins by giving a bit of a summary of his previous speeches, proclaiming God's power and justice and God's desire to draw people out of suffering. He warns Job not to let his suffering lead him into wrongdoing, charging him:

Watch yourself—don't turn to the iniquity
you seem to prefer to affliction!
        Job 36:21

After this summary, Elihu's tone begins to shift. He calls on Job to remember what God has done and recalls the praises of those who have witnessed God's mighty acts. The language and poetic syntax of Elihu's speech become elevated, verging on ecstatic praise, building to bridge the distance between human and divine by witnessing to the approaching thunderstorm, a shift captured well by the NIV translation of the passage:

At this my heart pounds
        and leaps from its place.
Listen! Listen to the roar of his voice,
        to the rumbling that comes from his mouth.
He unleashes his lightning beneath the whole heaven
        and sends it to the ends of the earth.
After that comes the sound of his roar;
        he thunders with his majestic voice.

When his voice resounds,
        he holds nothing back.
                Job 37:1-4 (NIV)

The subtle shift in Elihu's style is a powerful witness to the brilliance of the author's command of language, visible in the way the transition between the different styles is hardly noticeable until the atmosphere has changed entirely. The conclusion to Elihu's speeches introduces the thematic portrayal of the heavenly nature of God, using the imagery of a storm to speak to the wildness and power of God, and the imagery of the sky, and the sun's searing brightness, to speak of God's overwhelming majesty. His final speech to Job includes questions about God's character and glory that flow naturally into God's words in the divine speeches, and he is the one to transition the narrative into the tempestuous and glorious reality of a storm from the heavens.

Elihu seeks to witness to the true character of God, and his speeches conclude by drawing Job into the very presence of God. Job may be the one who stands before God in the following chapters, but the gap between his silence and the divine speeches is bridged by his unexpected young friend, Elihu. Through Elihu, the author reminds us of the truth that community and friendship are essential bridges to genuine healing and new life. Job does not stand as an isolated figure, casting his challenge into the void and then being answered by God. It is possible Job wouldn't have even heard God's answer if he hadn't been willing to listen to someone unexpected, someone younger than himself who confronted and challenged him.

Elihu's actions are the antithesis of Job's other three friends, who drive Job into a self-centered case against the perceived injustice of God. Their human wisdom was focused on human action and ended with Job issuing a self-centered and angry challenge to God. Elihu begins by witnessing to God, placing God, instead of Job, center-stage, and he concludes his speeches by ushering Job into the very presence of God. More than anything else, that larger arc distinguishes the character and nature of their friendship and their wisdom. Eliphaz, Bildad, and Zophar offered Job human wisdom, earthly wisdom drawn from their lived experience and traditional religious paradigms; Elihu speaks as one taught by the spirit of God, offering Job wisdom from above, wisdom that is found in who God truly is.

6

"I AM"

Job 38-42

The air thickens as a thunderstorm approaches, taking on a brownish hue; there is a silence and a stillness that echo something of the immense weight and whirling fury of the approaching storm. Dark clouds form and move across the sky. Flickers of lightning are answered by deep roars of thunder as the sense of sheer power and ferocity builds. There is a word in Hebrew that perhaps conveys this reality more fully than any word or phrase in English: *kavod*, commonly translated "glory," a word that derives its meaning from a sense of heaviness or weightiness. The charged air before a storm carries something of this tangible weight, bringing with it a sense of awe, power, and wonder—God draws near.

The Lord reigns, let the earth be glad;
let distant shores rejoice.
Clouds and thick darkness surround him;
righteousness and justice are the foundation of his throne.
Fire goes before him

and consumes his foes on every side.
His lightning lights up the world;
  the earth sees and trembles.
The mountains melt like wax before the Lord,
  before the Lord of all the earth.
The heavens proclaim his righteousness,
  and all peoples see his glory.
  Psalm 97:1-6 (NIV)

God's speeches in chapters thirty-eight through forty-one, spoken from within a raging thunderstorm, are spectacular portrayals of wildness and majesty. Descriptions of creation are used as mental stepping stones to God's grandeur, directing our attention to the surpassing wonder of creation and then opening up beyond this world to the God who made it all, and who is greater than even the most mysterious or powerful aspect of this universe. God unleashes a barrage of questions on Job, challenging him to answer:

The LORD answered Job out of the thunderstorm and said:

"Who is this darkening counsel
with words that fail knowledge?
Gird your loins like a warrior and answer me:

Where were you when I founded the earth?
Show me the place where you stood!
Who took its measurements—
        surely you know!
Who drew up its plans?
Into what were the foundations sunk?
Who set the cornerstone in place
        to the chorus of the morning stars,
        to the joyful shout of the sons of God?

Who held firm the doors to the sea
when it burst from the womb and came roaring out;
        when I wrapped it in clouds,
        and swaddled it with thunderstorms?
When I broke it to its place, and set bars and doors on it,
when I said, 'Up to here—no further!
Here your swelling waves stop!'

In all your days, have you ever commanded the morning?
Have you ever shown the dawn its place—
        that it might grab the earth by the edges
        to shake the wicked from it?
It takes shape like clay under a seal,
rises to its station like a garment;

light is withheld from the wicked,
their uplifted arm is broken."
Job 38:2-15

The questions God asks Job in the first portion of the divine speeches take him on a journey across the expanse of the earth and to the very limits of the created world. They start with the foundation of the earth and the birth of the sea, then move to the dawn, the deep places of the earth, the origins of light and darkness, the sky with its winds, rains, and storms, and the stars in the farthest heavens. The first portion of the speech is thematically concluded by a return to the earth, where God questions Job on his power to draw rain down from the heavens, bringing life and vitality to the plants and creatures of the earth.

The barrage of questions then continues with a more detailed focus on the wild creatures and ecosystems of the earth. God's initial questions served to establish the fundamental dimensions of creation; in the next portion of the speech, God proceeds to walk through the dizzying explosion of diversity encountered within the created world. God seems to revel in precisely the kind of creatures and places that seem most strange or bizarre to us as humans: dangerous carnivores, animals inhabiting remote and inaccessible locations, birds that do not seem to care properly for their young, war-horses exulting in the frenzy of battle, and predatory raptors soaring through the air. The images begin with lions crouching in their dens and end with eagles nesting in remote mountain peaks, reversing the overall trajectory of the speeches once again by moving from the earth back to the heavens. Just as God first took Job on a comprehensive journey through the dimensions of creation, God takes Job on a panoramic journey through the wild spaces of the earth, with the movement from earth to heaven giving God's descriptions a sense of comprehensiveness in portraying the wild animals and places of the earth:

Can you bring down prey for the lion
or sustain the life of the pride,
when they lie down in their dens,
or crouch in a thicket to stalk?

Do you know the proper birthing time,
the time for the labor pains of the mountain goats?
Do you watch the deer,
or count the months till they are full?
Do you know when they bear their young?

Who set the wild donkey free?
Who was it that loosed his bonds?
I made him a home in the desert plains,

with the salt flats as his dwelling place.
He laughs at the noise of the city,
and pays no mind to the shouts of a driver;
he roams the mountainside for pasture,
searching out every green thing.

Did you give the horse its strength?
Were you the one to clothe its neck with thunder?
Can you make him leap like a locust?
The splendor of his snorting strikes terror;
he paws the ground of the valley,
delighting in his strength
he charges into battle.
He laughs at fear, and is not dismayed,
he does not turn back from the sword.
Arrayed against him is the rattling quiver
the flaming tongue of spear and javelin;
with trembling anticipation he eats up the distance,
unable to wait when he hears the sound of the trumpet.

Is it by your wisdom that the hawk soars
and spreads its wings to the south?
It is at your word that the eagle rises
and nests in the heights?

It dwells on the side of a cliff,
its rocky teeth a fortress;
from there it searches out food,
eyes scanning from afar;
its chicks suckle on blood
and where the slain are—it is there.
        Job 38:39-40, 39:1-2, 5-8, 19-24, 26-30

After all these questions, Job covers his mouth, saying that he has no reply to God—but God is not finished yet. A second speech follows the first, where God questions Job about his power to enact justice and govern the world, and then describes two mythological beings, Behemoth and Leviathan. The fierce and predatory creatures which conclude God's first speech transition thematically to God's ability to enact justice in the world, providing a snapshot of God's ferocity and power. God asks Job whether he is able to bring down the proud and crush the wicked, or whether he has the power to save himself in bringing about justice and deliverance:

Would you annul my justice?
Would you declare me wicked, so that you can be right?
Do you have an arm like God,
or can your voice thunder like his?

Exalt yourself, then, in majesty,
clothe yourself in splendor and power!
Dispense the fury of your wrath:
> *see the proud and bring them low*
> *see the proud and subdue them*
> *crush the wicked to their place*
> *bury them in the dirt together*
> *hide their faces in the grave.*
Then I will acknowledge
that your own right hand can save you!
> Job 40:8-14

After questioning Job about his power to enact justice, God turns to the creatures Behemoth and Leviathan. Behemoth takes a form with echoes of a hippopotamus, one of the largest, strongest, and most dangerous of all creatures that dwell on land or in shallow waters:

Look at Behemoth,
which I made along with you;
he feeds on grass like cattle.
Look at the strength of his loins,
the power in his muscled stomach!
> *His tail bends like a cedar*
> *his sinews tighten—*

his core is molded in bronze,
his bones like rods of iron.

Under the lotus plant he lies,
concealed by the marshy reeds;
lotuses cover him with shade,
the willows of the stream surround him;
> *the river presses in—*
> *he remains confident, unperturbed,*
> *though the Jordan itself burst against his mouth!*
>> Job 40:15-18, 21-23

Behemoth is described as the chief of all freshwater creatures, preeminent on land among the created beings of God. Leviathan is the equivalent chief of all sea creatures, what we might think of as part crocodile and part mythological sea serpent. Leviathan was a creature who figured prominently in the mythology of cultures surrounding ancient Israel, its prominence witnessed by the way the imagery shows up in different parts of the Hebrew scriptures, like Psalm 74:14 and Isaiah 27:1. A common theme within the creation myths from cultures around ancient Israel involved a divine figure slaying a chaos monster like Leviathan and using its body to form the world. The author of Job takes the basic form of this idea and turns it on its head, placing the free and untamed chaos-monster Leviathan as the pinnacle of God's creation, a fearsome and dangerous creature, yet still part of God's created world:

When he rises up, the mighty flee,
before his crashing they all go astray.

Arrows cannot drive him away,
slingstones turn to chaff before him.
To him a club is like a piece of straw,
and he laughs at the shaking of the javelin.
His belly is sharp as broken pottery,
cutting tracks in the mud;
he boils the depths like a pot,
the sea he stirs like ointment;
his path glistens behind him,
as though the deep were crowned with white.
There is nothing of dust like him—
　　　　　made without fear.
He looks down on every high thing,
he is king over all the proud.
　　　　Job 41:25, 28-34

Behemoth and Leviathan are creatures that exhibit the power and wildness of creation, untamed by the human will, answerable to God alone. In some ways, the two creatures are opposites, their pairing meant to encompass the entirety of creation that lies between them. Behemoth is a freshwater creature, standing in a river, hidden from human eyes, while Leviathan is a sea creature, portrayed through motion and violent conflict with humanity. As Carol Newsom puts it, Behemoth plays "immovable object" to Leviathan's "irresistible force."[7] Leviathan in particular as a mythological sea creature would have been a terrifying and awe-inspiring figure to the ancient Israelite reader or listener. In Israelite culture and literature, sea imagery held specific connotations. The Mediterranean Sea, lying to the west of Israel, was often portrayed as an embodiment of the forces of chaos, shifting and ever-changing in contrast to firm and solid land. It is not a coincidence that the Hebrew word for "human" (*adam*) derives from a word meaning "earth" or "dirt"— we humans are earth-creatures, made from and sustained by the soil we walk upon. God's power in creation is often depicted in Hebrew poetry through the way God is able to still the raging seas or set boundaries for its wild and untamable nature.

As a mythological sea creature, Leviathan is the ultimate representation of the forces of wildness and chaos in the world. Its home in the sea is a place of supreme wildness, a place untamed by the human hand, with depths unexplored by even the most adventurous or daring. Leviathan answers only to God, and the idea of its domestication is laughable. Its mythological character connects it to the act of creation, and its presence in the divine speeches contrasts ironically with Job's initial lament, where he wished for someone to rouse Leviathan to destroy the day of his birth and undo God's creation. The cosmic creation imagery of chapter thirty-eight, the wild animals and ecosystems of chapter thirty-nine, the power of God in bringing down the wicked at the beginning of chapter forty, and Behemoth as "chief" of God's creatures are all drawn together thematically into one awe-inspiring entity for the culmination of God's speeches—Leviathan. In its particularity, Leviathan encompasses the totality of what has come before.

It might seem strange to find a description of a mythical creature serving as the pinnacle of God's speeches. In fact, the entire content of the speeches might seem strange at first and disconnected from the rest of the book of Job. However, a unique perspective is being conveyed through God's speeches, a perspective that stands in intentional contrast to the first half of the book. God's speeches draw a contrast between human wisdom and divine wisdom, seen through creation itself. The difference is striking when the domesticated animals from the beginning of the book are compared to the wild creatures that feature in the divine speeches. At the beginning of the book, Job is described along with his orderly flocks and herds. Job is prosperous and wealthy because of his animals, each domesticated and cultivated specifically to serve him, whether his need is food, wool, milk, transportation, or brute strength in tilling fields. According to a human-oriented perspective, those are proper creatures—sheep, camels, oxen, and donkeys—firmly under the control of humans and well-suited to meet their needs.

Here in the divine speeches, however, we are given a perspective that is vastly different from that anthropocentric conception of the world with its tame and productive animals. In the divine speeches, we are introduced to God's creatures and God's world. These wild beings and the dizzying diversity of ecosystems in which they live are a far cry from Job's orderly herds and productive fields. God's creatures roam the wilderness untamed, taking a bewildering variety of forms: lions, ravens, mountain goats, wild donkeys and oxen, ostriches, hawks, and eagles. These are creatures that defy conventional wisdom in raising their young, dangerous carnivores on the hunt, predatory raptors who reside in inaccessible mountain eyries, and terrifying sea monsters. God's wisdom is not our wisdom; there is something of God reflected in every creature in the divine speeches, even the terrifying, the confusing, and the awe-inspiring figures. These creatures thrive in the wilderness, the region of exile beyond human society where Job located himself in his case against God.

Job wants to be restored to his conception of human fullness, placed once again at the center of society and of the human world, but God seems thoroughly uninterested in doing so. Job envisons a world that revolves around him and his needs, but through these wild creatures God reminds him that creation fundamentally reflects God, not Job. Though it is true that Job has been cast to the fringes of human society because of his suffering, that does not mean that Job is at the fringes of God's world. Instead of restoring Job to his former place, God is intent on drawing Job into a larger story, moving him towards a different kind of restoration.

A vital aspect of the divine speeches is the resolution of the ongoing theme of a legal case or test of character, an interpretive framework that has already changed and developed within the story. At the beginning of the book, Job's character and faith were put on trial through a divine test, staged as a competition between God and the Accuser. By the end of the first half of the book, Job had turned the tables on God and staged his own trial, putting God's character and apparent faithlessness to the test. Finally, at the end of the book, God shows up in answer to Job's case as defendant, and yet in doing so takes the role of questioner. God's defense consists of Job being asked question after question. These questions are not a form of divine bullying, as some have suggested, as though God were trying to put Job in his proper place as a mere mortal. To read God's speeches in that way is to miss the wonder and profound self-revelation within the speeches. Through the divine speeches, Job does not come to a greater knowledge of the workings of the divine as something he can demonstrate mastery or control over, a reality that remains the constant irony behind God's questions and the portrayal of wild and undomesticated creatures. Instead, he comes to know God, and his response is to cover his mouth and profess his awestruck ignorance.

The story of Job began with the idea that Job's faith was being tested by God through his experience of suffering. His suffering was portrayed as a necessary evil, since there was no way God could know in advance if Job would remain faithful once God's blessing and protection were removed from his life, no way to tell whether Job truly loved or followed God "without reason." In the divine speeches at the end of the book, however, Job's test is rearticulated, portrayed not as a challenge of maintaining faith in God in the midst of horrific circumstances, but rather as his response to the revelation of God. Here we see the author's use of narrative misdirection come full circle, the "aha!" moment reached with the climactic revelation of God: Job's faith, as a measure of the strength of his character and religious conviction in the face of profound suffering, is no longer the central point around which the plot of the story revolves.

As readers and listeners, we thought that the outcome of the story would be determined by Job's response to God in reaction to his experience of suffering. That whole paradigm and explanation, though, was a set-up on the part of the author, and the nature of faith is reinterpreted as the book moves from a starting point that is human-oriented, centered on Job, to one that is divine-oriented, centered on the revelation of God. The book of Job began with the driving question of whether Job's faith in God would be strong enough to withstand the tragic and senseless events that occurred; it ends with the question of whether Job is willing to lay aside his case against God to embrace what God is in the process of doing.

Faith in the deepest and truest sense is not about human effort and moral endurance in the midst of extreme difficulty. In the deepest and truest sense, faith is about human response to the revelation of God. One perspective places humanity at the center and origin of faith, while the other sees God as the initiator. The contrast is striking when the two halves of the story are held up against one another in comparison. Each half reflects the other like a mirror, but unlike a true reflection, the conclusion to the book of Job takes each of the elements present in the first half of the book and reflects them in a profoundly altered way. The two divine council scenes at the beginning of the book, comprised of dialogue between God and the Accuser, are mirrored by two speeches of self-revelation given by God to Job; Job's two initial responses at the beginning of the book, highlighting his own endurance and faith, are replaced by two responses to the revealed majesty of God; the question of how Job will respond to his suffering—framed as a revelation of his true character—is replaced by the revelation of God's true character.

This conceptual reinterpretation of faith is paralleled by a subtle shift in the whole paradigm of interacting with the divine. At the beginning of the story, there is a clear and unbroken division between earth and heaven, human and divine. God is in heaven, Job is on earth, and the relationship between them is comprised of Job making sacrifices to God, and God speaking about Job to the heavenly council. In the final chapters of the book, there are two speeches in which God is revealed from heaven, speaking to Job from the midst of a thunderstorm, utterly demolishing that initial chasm between heaven and earth. The God that Job encounters at the end of the book is a God who comes near, a God who speaks—not *about* Job, but *to* Job. Job encounters a God who is mighty and awesome beyond his wildest imagining, and yet who chooses to be revealed to him, initiating a new kind of divine-human relationship and altering the entire direction of Job's narrative.

Job has been stuck inside all-too-human systems of thought and reasoning, stuck in the idea that God has unjustly wronged him, and that—as makes sense to us in a tame and easily comprehensible universe—he deserves recompense for those wrongs. God is intent on breaking through this superficial perspective in order to draw Job out of his profoundly self-centered conception of the world. As Robert Alter notes in *The Art of Biblical Poetry*, the poetic images comprising God's speeches are set in intentional contrast to the imagery from Job's speeches and his case against God, particularly from his initial lament in chapter three.[8] Job responded to his suffering by cursing both the day of his birth and the joyful shout which was the response to his conception, wishing that it would never see the light of day; it is no accident that some of the first images of the divine speeches include the "joyful shout" of the sons of God in creation, God acting as midwife to the birth of the sea, and the dawn of a new day. Job's lament was inward-focused, intent on shutting out light and life because of the profound pain and suffering he had experienced. He expressed a longing for the rest that would come with death, framed as freedom from toil and misery. In contrast to Job's inward-turning lament, through the divine speeches God invites Job into a radical expanding of perspective, an embrace of life and light and everything in existence even to the very ends of the oceans. God is pulling Job into a larger story and a different kind of freedom, inviting Job into a new way of relating with the world.

Through this dynamic invitation, we receive the author's profound wisdom regarding human suffering. Rather than an explanation, we receive a revelation. Instead of being given a reason for the tragic events of Job's life, we are given a God who breaks down the barrier between heaven and earth to know and be known. In Job's story we are never given an answer to the question of his suffering. Job has experienced terrible suffering and is fully capable of holding on to that fact, turning inward in pain and anguish, self-justified until his dying day. The only answer to his suffering comes in the revelation of God, and in Job giving himself over to the God who brings light out of darkness and life out of death, allowing himself to be drawn anew into the wild and dangerous world which God delights in.

Job's response to God's speeches is to withdraw his case and turn to God in renewed and transformed faith. Rather than remaining in a world that revolves around his pain and suffering, he chooses to step into God's ongoing story of re-creation. His choice to do so is far more impressive than his lifetime of religious diligence up to that point. It is a choice that perhaps not everyone would make. The final words of Job—his actual last words in the book—come in 42:1-6, where Job witnesses to the God he has now seen and come to know:

Job answered the LORD and said:

"I know that you are able to do all things,
and that nothing can thwart your purpose.
'Who is this that veils counsel without knowledge?'
*   Surely I spoke of things I did not understand,*

things too wondrous for me, which I did not know.
'Listen—I will speak, and you will answer me:'
    My ear had heard of you,
    but now my eye has seen you.

Therefore I reject myself, and repent of dust and ashes."
    Job 42:1-6

There is some ambiguity present in these lines, and different ways in which Job's final words could be translated. The NRSV translation of Job 42:6 reads:

"therefore I despise myself,
and repent in dust and ashes."
    Job 42:6 (NRSV)

However, this translation can be misleading because it gives a sense of Job simply acknowledging his state as a sinful mortal before the power and glory of God. The common translation choice of the word "despise" is particularly misleading, since the main force of the Hebrew root is to reject or cast off, rather than to hold in a state of continual contempt. In these final words, Job chooses to cast off his self-centered case and perspective, saying: "I had it wrong. I was operating based on what I had heard of God—but now that I have met God, and seen God, my case is no longer relevant, and I choose to reject it and turn to God." Job abandons his case against God, while also leaving behind his condition of mourning in dust and ashes, having received God's self-revelation. Job humbles himself before God, choosing to loosen his grip on his own suffering and pain. He has met the God who, far from being a maniacal tyrant hell-bent on shattering his life in a divinely ordained test of faith, is a God who has drawn near and spoken to him, who has been revealed as far more mysterious and awesome and wild than he had imagined.

Somewhere in the midst of this revelation of a wild God who is free and unconstrained by mere human wisdom, Job is able to let go of his pain, his religious anxiety, and his strictly ordered, human-oriented view of the world. All of the creation imagery from the divine speeches culminates in the new creation that occurs within Job's own life. Although Job's experience of suffering is neither erased nor forgotten, he is nevertheless able to move forward into the new thing God brings into being. He is able to have children again, risking further devastation and suffering by extending himself in love:

The LORD *blessed the following days of Job's life more than his beginning: he had fourteen thousand sheep, six thousand camels, a thousand pairs of oxen, and a thousand donkeys;*

and he had seven sons, and three daughters. His first daughter he called Jemimah, the second Keziah, and the third Keren-Happuch. In all the land you could not find women more beautiful than Job's daughters, and Job gave them an inheritance along with their brothers.

Job 42:12-15

The conclusion to Job's life, as he is blessed by God with children and his possessions are multiplied, is easy to gloss over, or to misunderstand. At first glance, it might seem like the book of Job comes full circle, with Job's life returning to what it was before, only in a greater degree of material blessing, with God restoring Job's former life in recompense for the suffering that was inflicted on him. However, the narrative has shifted in subtle ways, and the Job we see at the end of the book is not the same character he was at the beginning of the book. Healing from suffering is never simply reduced to replacing what was lost—some things will never return. Job might have the gift of new children, but that does not change the reality of his loss, or the grief that will remain with him for the rest of his life. Jerry Sittser, reflecting on his own experience of loss in the book *A Grace Disguised*, compares it to the sensation of a missing limb and the "phantom pain" that is often felt.[9] Even if the wound heals, something will always be missing, and that reality doesn't go away. That doesn't mean, though, that there is any less goodness or fullness to the new life found in God, the ever-creative God who brings renewal into being in the most unexpected of ways. Job's renewed and increased abundance, rather than being a reward or replacement for what was lost, is meant to symbolize the richness of life that can be found despite a profound loss that will always remain. It is a seemingly paradoxical reality, represented symbolically by the author through Job's doubled abundance. Job's life is not the same; somehow, it is even fuller in spite of the loss and suffering he has experienced, a mystery and a miracle that only God can account for.

When reading the conclusion of the book alongside Job's introduction, some noticeable differences emerge. One is the complete absence of religious anxiety in Job's life. At the beginning of the book, Job is portrayed as getting up early every day to sacrifice for his children just in case one of them "blessed" God in the secrecy of their own heart. Part of this religious anxiety likely derived from Job's conception of God, which the author portrayed through the literary device of mirroring human and divine. When the story began, the figure of God was in many ways a reflection of Job. Just as Job is the greatest person in all the east, God is the greatest being in the heavens; just as Job worries about the condition of his children's hearts, and what kind of "blessing" they give to God, God is unsure about Job and what kind of "blessing" he is truly giving to God. The conception of God as a reflection of humanity was also present in Job's final case, made in chapters twenty-nine through thirty-one, where Job appealed to God's justice as a divine version of the human social and moral ideal that he held. If God was righteous, God was required to act like Job as a benevolent patron and vindicate the innocent, restoring him to his place of honor and abundance.

After encountering God through the divine speeches at the end of the book, there is a tangible freedom to the lack of concern in Job's spiritual life. Rather than God being a reflection of human ideals, Job's life becomes a reflection of God. He has met God, and now he knows God, the living God, wild and majestic and good beyond anything he could have imagined. At the end of the book, there is no parallel to his anxious habit of getting up early every morning to offer sacrifices for his children. Having met God, Job isn't worried about messing up the minutiae of his religious life, as though God were waiting for a single misstep to bring calamity down upon him. He has also grown into a character who couldn't care less about the superficial social norms or religious expectations of his time that are grounded in human wisdom and traditions. He gives an inheritance to his daughters along with his sons, an act which would have been shocking in his context, upending traditional power structures and gender norms. Giving an inheritance to his daughters would have been perceived as dangerous to the social conceptions of those around him, but

Job's life is noticeably free in a way that it was not at the beginning of the book, a reality that reflects the freedom of the God he has encountered.

Job has embraced wisdom "from above," choosing to center his life not on the suffering he has experienced, but on the revelation of the God who delights in every living thing for its own sake, not just for how it fits into human norms or ideals. Job is operating out of a different way of seeing the world, one which is not bound by human hierarchies and structures of power, but which derives from the delight and care God shows to each living creature. The difference is visible in the shift in focus from Job's sons at the beginning of the book to Job's daughters at the end of the book. At the beginning of the story, the focus of Job's actions and the author's description of his family life was on Job's sons and the feasts they would each hold, an emphasis that makes sense in the patriarchal culture of Job's time. The book ends, though, with Job lavishing attention on his daughters, giving each of them unique and beautiful names. Naming someone in a Hebrew scriptural text is an act loaded with meaning, a significance that might be difficult for us to grasp today. It demonstrates identity and importance, and it is likely no accident that Job's three young daughters take the place of Eliphaz, Bildad, and Zophar—Job's three named and socially prominent older male friends—at the end of the book. Job no longer lives in a world in which human society and hierarchy determine value and importance; he lives in God's world, a world filled with all kinds of diverse creatures and people that God delights in simply for being what they were created to be.

Just before these descriptions of Job's renewed and transformed life, there is a scene in which God speaks to Job's three friends in an ironic reversal of their collective argument against Job:

After the LORD *spoke these words to Job, the* LORD *said to Eliphaz the Temanite: "My wrath burns against you and your two friends, for you have not spoken rightly of me like my servant Job has. Now take seven bulls and seven rams and go to my servant Job and offer a burnt offering for yourselves; my servant Job shall intercede for you, and I will accept his prayer not to deal with you according to your folly, for you have not spoken rightly of me like my servant Job has." So Eliphaz the Temanite and Bildad the Shuhite and Zophar the Naamathite went and did as the* LORD *commanded them, and the* LORD *accepted Job's prayer.*

Job 42:7-9

Job's three friends made many extended and passionate speeches trying to convince Job that he was hiding some egregious sin that he needed to reveal and confess. At the end of the book, God reveals that they are the ones who need to act to redress their wrongdoing—the fact that they did not speak truly of God, in contrast to Job. The three sages are humbled, and must ask Job to intercede for them, a complete reversal from their previous state of supposed wisdom. God's affirmation of Job's words is striking, since Job's speeches were filled with blasphemous accusations and agonized searching. God says that Job's way of speaking is the right one, the correct response to suffering. The friends, on the other hand, receive God's rebuke for trying to fit Job's experience into their limited religious paradigm of sin and retributive justice.

After Job intercedes for his three friends and receives gifts from his family and extended community to begin life anew, we are told that God blesses Job:

The LORD blessed the following days of Job's life more than his beginning....
    Job 42:12a

If we think back to the beginning of the book, we were waiting expectantly to see whether Job would bless God or "bless" God. When we reach the end of the book and witness Job's climactic encounter with God, we find that neither happens. Job does not bless God, in either sense of the word. There is no final scene revisiting the divine council in which Job is demonstrated to be victorious and faithful on God's behalf, no conclusion to the contest between God and the Accuser. By the end of Job's story, that problematic paradigm has been replaced by a reality that is both simpler and more mysterious: *the LORD blessed the following days of Job's life....* The driving question of Job's story is no longer about whether Job will bless God; it is about God's blessing of Job, and whether Job is willing to accept and live into the blessing that God is actively extending to him, despite his inexplicable experience of suffering. It is by receiving and living into the blessing of God that Job is able to live into God's ongoing story of creation and rebirth, and into the revelation of the God who brings new life out of devestation and death.

By the end of the book, the center of gravity in Job's life has shifted. The story is no longer about the strength of Job's faith in God, or about Job receiving recompense for his suffering or an answer for his pain. Instead, it is about what God is doing, and how Job is living into that new creation. There is still never an explanation given for Job's suffering. For many people this fact might be puzzling or infuriating. The neat and tidy explanations of the workings of the divine given at the beginning of the book were systematically deconstructed, and when rearticulated in the second half of the book what replaces those explanations is simply God—the God who speaks and blesses, who acts and who is revealed. Job's human story, with its tame and predictable God, and its comprehensible universe reflecting human wisdom, has become God's story, wild and vibrant, a story not centered on what has happened to Job but on God's revelation and re-creation. It is a story that ends with the new life God speaks into existence; as the thunderstorm fades and the sky clears, there is perhaps a tangible lightness to the air, with a scent of vibrant freshness that hints at the new life just beginning.

Afterword

Between the book of Job and our modern world lies a vast chasm of history and cultural difference. The experience of suffering, though, continues to be a reality as prevalent today as when the book of Job was written, and the nature of suffering and the difficult questions it raises have not changed. Tracing Job's character arc across the entire book provides a profound glimpse into the nature of both suffering and healing, one that can speak to us today and help guide us as we grapple with our own experiences of suffering.

The portrayal of Job's response to suffering in the book follows a pattern common to human experiences of suffering and loss. At first, Job's response is to try and hold the norms and beliefs of his life together, responding automatically, perhaps in a state of shock:

Naked I came from my mother's womb,
and naked I shall return there.
The LORD gave, and the LORD has taken away;
blessed be the name of the LORD.
        Job 1:21

Job's initial expression of faith then shifts to deep pain and despair as he begins to process the reality of what has happened to him. It takes a full week of silence, sitting with his three friends who have come to support and console him, before he is able to speak. When he does speak, his words express all-encompassing anguish as he gives voice to his pain and curses his own existence. Job's process of moving from despair and dislocation into healing is hampered by Eliphaz, Bildad, and Zophar, who introduce simplistic narratives about sin and retributive justice, but is aided by Elihu, who cuts through those superficial arguments and points Job toward the truth about who God is. Walking into newness and healing requires Job to embrace life anew in all its complexity, mystery, pain, and wonder, and to choose to live out of a larger narrative not centered on himself. An essential step in healing for Job was to stop revolving around the pain of his own suffering and instead to step out courageously into the uncertainties and possibilities of a world that is wild and dangerous and yet still profoundly beautiful and good.

Job's story is our collective story as human beings who live in a world fraught with suffering and pain. His story invites us as readers and listeners into the vibrant renewal of life that can be experienced even after unspeakable tragedy. The fact that the author of Job is able to reflect such a universal reality speaks to the literary power and spiritual depth of the book. The book of Job will always remain one of the great classics of world literature, a story that belongs to everyone, not only to those who profess a faith in God or hold it as inspired scripture. Though written from the perspective of God's revelation to the people of Israel, the author of Job chose to set the story in the distant past with a protagonist who is not an Israelite, in a time before Israel's covenant relationship with God. God's revelation in the book also happens primarily through the lens of creation and wilderness, a portrayal that opens up the possibility for anyone to follow Job in his journey of healing toward a renewed fullness of life. Job's story of suffering and healing can truly be anyone's story, anyone who is willing to walk alongside him down into the valley of suffering and be drawn up the other side into new life.

Perhaps the best place for us to begin in following the courageous example of Job in dealing with our own experiences of suffering is in speaking truth boldly and freely—truth about the evils of this world, truth about our own situations, and truth about our own struggle. That truth is spoken first and foremost to God and is one of the most honest forms of prayer there is, a fact that is all too often forgotten or obscured. It might be tempting to focus on the end of Job's story and to think that it is possible to gloss over the rest, all the pain and despair that Job expresses, but there is a reason that Job was not written as a series of divine speeches in isolation providing the theological "answer" to the problem of suffering. Job's expression of pain, his agonized search for an adequate explanation for his suffering, and his searing accusations of God are essential steps on his journey toward healing. God's response to Job's raw and honest emotional expression is to affirm that Job's response is the proper one. We sometimes tend to fear being honest with God—or even with ourselves—and yet we witness God hearing Job's accusations, Job's challenge, even Job's claim that unless God vindicates him, God is less righteous than Job, and God says at the end of the book that Job is the one who has spoken truly. It is Job's friends, Eliphaz, Bildad, and Zophar, in trying to correct Job's experience with rationalized religious platitudes and limited theological perspectives, who receive God's rebuke.

Job's expression of truth did not necessarily involve the correct idea of God or understanding of what was going on. Rather, his truthfulness was expressed through the fact that he spoke to God from his own experience with utter honesty and with a genuine openness to hearing God and the perspectives of others. He was willing to hear God, and even to lay aside his own way of thinking and understanding when necessary. Job's questions were not a way for him to hide, cynical in attitude, spinning out unanswerable queries to prevent a real encounter with God. Job could have used his doubts and pain to reject God, or he could have held his questions back, refusing to challenge or question God out of a sense of misplaced piety, but he didn't. Instead, Job chose to express his pain and suffering fully, bringing it out into the open. Job chose to be vulnerable in his suffering, crying out for God, unsatisfied with unsatisfying answers and unwilling to quit until he had made his case in full and heard the response of God.

Job's story also reminds us of the vitally important role of community in the context of expressing suffering and journeying towards healing. The impact of Job's friends on him, and their role in the story, is complex. Eliphaz, Bildad, and Zophar initially provided the necessary compassionate presence that enabled Job to give voice to his deep grief and pain, but then became locked in conflict with him due to limited theological perspectives. Despite their combative tone, though, it is in conversation with them that Job is able to clarify his own thoughts and fully express his own pain. Elihu provides a different perspective as he rebukes Job, reminding him of the true nature of God. Elihu does not simply tell Job that he is wrong. He confronts Job's distorted image of God and does his best to point him in the right direction, which is first and foremost toward the truth about God. Elihu provides an example of a positive response to those who have suffered, but a response of anger like the one he offers requires a nuanced understanding of the situation and a sensitivity to others which are not easily achieved. There are things to learn from each of the characters in the story.

As human beings, we are fundamentally relational, and we need to work out our healing in the context of a community that can confront us with both compassion and correction. Job was not alone, and his journey happened in relationship with others, some of it harmful and some of it helpful. Job does not come to new life by standing alone before the unapproachable majesty of God and casting his defiant questions out into the void, but rather is able to voice his suffering in the compassionate presence of his three friends, and finds a new direction through his willingness to listen to the wisdom of Elihu, someone he could have easily silenced or dismissed as young, impetuous, or inferior.

While the role of the friends in Job's journey is complicated, certain perspectives are fully rejected. The two dominant paradigms of thought the author introduces and then deconstructs in the first half of the book—the tendency to identify suffering as a divine test, or to rationalize the experience of suffering by trying to discern what "caused" it—are examples of damaging and unhelpful ways of responding to others who have suffered. The question "whose fault was this?" or the desire to give meaning to an otherwise inexplicable experience by imputing agency to God with some ultimately benevolent motive continue to be basic human reactions to the experience of suffering. The book of Job should serve as a resounding reminder to avoid falling into the trap of either giving a rational explanation or trying to find a divinely ordained reason for either our own, or someone else's, experience of suffering, and to avoid trying to provide a facile affirmation that if only certain steps or actions were taken things would be quickly resolved: "if only you prayed more...if only you hadn't made those poor choices...if only you worked harder...if only you had more faith... then all of this wouldn't have happened to you, or would be quickly resolved, or at least wouldn't be affecting you in this way." Those are the kinds of responses voiced by Eliphaz, Bildad, and Zophar that receive God's rebuke at the end of Job, and which are shattered by the revelation of the awesome and mysterious nature of God in the divine speeches.

In responding to the reality of human suffering, the story of Job points us toward a transformative encounter, instead of a rational answer to our questions. In Job we never get a "why;" instead, we get a "who." And yet the glory, the holiness, and the majesty of that "who" is enough to knock Job right off his feet, enough to cause him to place his hand over his mouth and say:

My ear had heard of you, but now my eye has seen you.
        Job 42:5

Through Job's encounter with God, we see that our questions, rather than being answered, are transformed. There is new life for those willing to step outside of their own pain and encounter the living God. Job's encounter with God is spiritual in the deepest sense, but it is not one he experiences through the religious practices of his time or the theological paradigms of Eliphaz, Bildad, and Zophar. He encounters the God of life, the God whose wisdom is reflected in the dazzling beauty and bizarre contradictions of nature. Suffering itself is never explained in the book of Job. The problematic paradigms offered at the beginning of the book explaining why Job suffered are systematically deconstructed by Job's resolute honesty, and the only thing that replaces them at the end of the book is the active presence and words of the living God, with Job choosing to live into the new life and blessing that is extended to him. That may not sound like a satisfying answer to the problem of suffering and evil in the world. It is not a philosophical answer; it is an answer that must be lived, an answer that rests on faith and surrender. It is an answer that abandons wisdom "from below" and embraces the fullness of God and the new life that is offered "from above," and only the lived journey of transformation itself will reveal if it is answer enough.

The way the book of Job ends, having deconstructed some common reasons given to explain human suffering, and then refusing to replace those explanations with anything but the creative power and presence of God, is perhaps the most difficult part of the book to wrestle with. As human beings we crave explanations. We want things to make sense, to be explainable, to be something that we can comprehend. Even bad reasons used to explain suffering can be more comforting than no reason at all. That is part of why the first half of the book of Job and the full expression of his agony is so important. Job refuses to hide his pain or take the easy way out by covering over his suffering with simplistic explanations. Job's brutal honesty is a central part of his journey toward healing, an insight into human nature that modern psychology would emphatically affirm. The journey of healing from trauma or loss does not involve forgetting, rationalizing, or ignoring the experience, but instead occurs through intentional exposure to it by bringing it out into the open, perhaps in the context of expressing it verbally to others, or perhaps by addressing it indirectly through a form of artistic expression.

Job needed to speak his case, to give voice to his suffering all the way to the "end" of his words. Job's expression of his pain lays the foundation for everything that follows, including his own openness to the revelation of God and his ability to walk into the new life that is extended to him. That new life doesn't make the suffering he has experienced vanish; when it comes to healing from trauma and suffering, the experience and the memories won't ever just go away, a reality that is important to keep in sight when reading the conclusion to Job's story. However, through honest and painful expression, suffering and pain can lose the power to define a person's life. What changes is not the experience itself, or even the memory of it, but the ability to move beyond the cycle of pain into something new and beautiful and good.

Job's response to God reminds us that after giving voice to our own suffering we must also choose to live into the blessing of a God who is involved in re-creation. That kind of growth and change doesn't just happen on its own and often involves discarding limited or self-centered perspectives. After God's revelation to Job in the thunderstorm, Job didn't have to choose to turn to God or embrace transformation. He could have stayed in his experience of suffering, rejecting the help of those around him and refusing to step into the new thing that God was doing. Job, however, chose courageously to step into new life. He came to know God, and after that transformative encounter, he began living his life in accordance with a new pattern. Job ceased viewing God as a reflection of his own image and abandoned the religious anxiety which came from that image of God. By the end of the story, he is free to live out a life that is a response to, and a reflection of, an awe-inspiring God who is wild and free.

One of the most remarkable things about the end of the book is that Job's renewal is lived out in the everyday and the ordinary, in family and community. Job does not become a mystic, living in a cave and contemplating the mystery of God, nor does he start a new religious movement. He also doesn't turn into the kind of heroic figure we might expect from the climax of a literary epic, one who is now able to overcome whatever difficulty or conflict his story involved through new insight and maturity. Instead of Job stepping into the role of redemptive hero, God has become the main character of the book, the center of Job's story, with Job now living out his own life as one small but cherished part of God's much larger world.

The book began as a story about Job; it ends as a story about God. The difference is seen through Job himself, who is transformed from the human ideal of his time to someone whose life has become a reflection of the God he has come to know in freedom and joy, someone who alters human-oriented social norms and lives a life free of religious anxiety, a life of inexplicable fullness and richness that somehow flows out of an experience of intense suffering and pain. That fullness and richness are reflected by a symbolic doubling of the normal human life expectancy as the book ends, with Job portraying the new and vibrant life that is extended to each one of us in the midst of a broken and suffering world:

After this Job lived for a hundred and forty years, and saw his children, and his children's children, to the fourth generation. And Job died, old and full of days.
Job 42:16-17

Endnotes:

1. Alter, Robert. *The Art of Biblical Poetry* (Revised edition. Basic Books: 2011) 92.

3. Newsom, Carol A. *The Book of Job: A Contest of Moral Imaginations* (Oxford University Press: 2003) 58.

4. Kushner, Harold S. *The Book of Job: When Bad Things Happened to a Good Person*. (Shocken Books: 2012) 51.
   I agree with Harold Kushner (as he references the Anchor Bible commentary) that the opening to Job's lament is best conveyed by the imprecatory "damn." There might be those who are made uncomfortable by the presence of profanity in a scriptural translation, or who object that it reads into the text a nuance to the Hebrew that isn't there, but I still think it is the best option available for capturing the spirit of Job's lament.

5. Newsom, *The Book of Job*, 101.

6. Lewis, C.S. *A Grief Observed* (HarperOne, 1994) 7.

7. Dostoevsky, Fyodor. *The Brothers Karamazov* (Trans. Richard Pevear and Larissa Volokhonsky. 12th edition. Farrar, Straus and Giroux: 2002) 245. Italics in original.

8. Newsom, *The Book of Job*, 250.

9. Alter, *The Art of Biblical Poetry*, 120-30.

10. Sittser, Jerry L. *A Grace Disguised: How the Soul Grows through Loss* (Zondervan: 1996) 73.

Acknowledgements

One person deserves acknowledgment more than anyone else for their many contributions to this book—and that is my partner and love, Hanna. It is no exaggeration to say that this book would not exist without her. She was the one who first showed me how to read Job with an eye to misdirection, and by doing so, made it possible for me to come to a good interpretation of a difficult text I had grappled with but never really understood. The insights and applications of this book have all been sharpened by her helpful criticisms and suggestions, and her artwork has given visual life to the book. Fittingly, the most pivotal conversations between us took place while hiking in stunning wilderness locations: in northern California in the summer of 2019 at Redwoods National Park, and in the Collegiate Peaks Wilderness of Colorado in the summer of 2020. Hanna was both the first reader and the most consistent editor of this book and has been a constant encouragement to me throughout. Thank you. For everything.

Though I am trying to offer a novel contribution to the interpretation of Job in this book, I am also aware of the inescapable reality of only being able to do so by standing on the shoulders of many, many readers and interpreters of Job who have together left behind a rich history of reflection. In order to make this book more streamlined, and to prevent unnecessary clutter and distraction, I have generally chosen only to provide references for direct quotations. However, I do want to give several authors who have profoundly influenced my reading of Job their due, authors whose work in many cases lies directly behind the interpretation I give at different points.

The first of these is Ellen Davis and the book *Getting Involved with God: Rediscovering the Old Testament* (Cowley Publications: 2001), particularly chapter ten, 'The Sufferer's Wisdom.' Davis' writing on the wild creatures of the divine speeches at the end of the book, and especially the freedom of Job in coming to reflect a God of joy and wildness, had a significant impact on me, sparking a renewed interest for me in the story of Job and laying part of the initial conceptual groundwork for the contrast of "God as a reflection of Job"/"Job as a reflection of God" in my own interpretation.

Carol Newsom's *The Book of Job: A Contest of Moral Imaginations* (Oxford University Press: 2003) has probably had a greater impact on my reading of Job than any other book. Newsom reads Job as a dialogic and multivocal expression of truth, and while that is not a reading I adopt or agree with, it gives Newsom's interpretation an impressive level of close attention to the different forms of expression utilized in Job. Several of Newsom's insights that were particularly influential on my reading deserve mention, such as the comprehensiveness of Job's initial poetic responses to his suffering, the narrative form of the paradigm behind the speeches of Eliphaz, Bildad, and Zophar, the spatial and hierarchical shape of Job's moral and social world in his final case against God, and the idea of God's speeches as a reversal of the creation motif of triumph over a chaos-monster.

Robert Alter's book *The Art of Biblical Poetry* (Revised edition: Basic Books: 2011) brilliantly illustrates the poetic contrast between Job's lament in chapter three and God's speeches in chapters thirty-nine through forty-one; as a literary critic Alter is incisive, and the way he draws out the contrast between the two forms of poetry helped my own articulation, although the historical-critical perspective which causes him to view the book as a composite rather than an intricately structured unity prevents him from pushing this insight further into the kind of mirrored structure which I argue for. Alter's translation in *The Wisdom Books: Job, Proverbs, and Ecclesiastes: A Translation with Commentary* (W. W. Norton & Company: 2011) was also helpful in illuminating some of the nuances of the Hebrew text, particularly in chapter eleven and Zophar's allusion to Job's "blemished" face.

Gustavo Gutiérrez's book *On Job: God-Talk and the Suffering of the Innocent* (Orbis Books: 1987) was an important influence in expanding my own understanding and perspective on how Job's own suffering opened his eyes to the suffering of others, particularly the poor and oppressed of the world, an important facet of Job's own journey and growth that deserves more emphasis and expansion than I was able to give it in this book. Jerry Sittser's book *A Grace Disguised: How the Soul Grows Through Loss* (Zondervan: 1996) charted a real-life example of what suffering and healing look like in the context of faith, and had a profound influence on my ideas about suffering.

Finally, Francis Anderson's excellent and accessible commentary *Job: An Introduction and Commentary* (IVP Academic: 1976) provided me with my first real taste of the power of the Hebrew poetry of Job, having read it before studying Hebrew myself. Anderson's translation of small portions of Job showed me the capacity of that kind of translation to capture the force of the poetry, and helped push me to provide my own translations in an effort to attempt something similar.

Many of those who generously offered me encouragement, reviews, and their editing expertise also deserve acknowledgement: Matthew Goodale, Isaac Quezada, Jerry Sittser, Nathan Daniels, David Robinson, Nathan Seppi, Deb and Tom Abbott, and Bill and Doris Mengel. They were part of the community which helped bring this book to life, and have my heartfelt gratitude.